You Can Go Home Again

"It is the darkness of misapprehension of God that is enshrouding the world. Men are losing their knowledge of His character. It has been misunderstood and misinterpreted. At this time a message from God is to be proclaimed, a message illuminating in its influence and saving in its power. His character is to be made known. Into the darkness of the world is to be shed the light of His glory, the light of His goodness, mercy, and truth."—Ellen G. White, *Christ's Object Lessons*, p. 415.

You Can Go Home Again

Jack Provonsha

Review and Herald Publishing Association
Washington, D.C.

Copyright © 1982 by
Review and Herald Publishing Association

This book was
Edited by Gerald Wheeler
Designed by Wendell Hill

Printed in U.S.A.

Library of Congress Cataloging in Publication Data

Provonsha, Jack W.
   You can go home again.
   1. Atonement.   2. Seventh-day Adventists—Doctrinal and controversial works.   I. Title.
BT265.2.P76   232'.3   81-23509
ISBN 0-8280-0098-0   AACR2

Contents

Preface
Chapter 1   Hostile or Friendly?   11
Chapter 2   The Crucial Question   18
Chapter 3   Is "Free" a Bargain?   23
Chapter 4   *Cur Deus Homo?*   27
Chapter 5   What Price Justice?   33
Chapter 6   Treasure in Earthen Vessels   44
Chapter 7   Clouded Windows   51
Chapter 8   The Darkness Behind the Shadows   60
Chapter 9   Fig Leaves for the Naked   77
Chapter 10   A Truth Disclosed   85
Chapter 11   Aids to Faith   97
Chapter 12   Tending the Garden   106
Chapter 13   You *Can* Go Home Again   112

Preface

How can one possibly justify the writing of another book on this subject? Surely the literally thousands of theological tomes and treatises produced over the many centuries since theologizing became a respectable discipline in the Christian church have adequately explored every nook and cranny of the idea of atonement. Perhaps so. But since the theme involves the issues that center on the very nature of God, surely it would be an act of superarrogance to suggest that human thought processes could ever exhaust it.

Besides, this is an "un-theology" of the atonement. Calling it an un-theology does not mean that we will be able to avoid at least some theology. What it does mean is that the book does not seek to be merely another attempt at analysis or at conceptual clarity regarding God's saving act. Basically it is a confession of faith. As such it participates in the grand chorus of praise John described in Revelation 5:11-13:

> And I beheld, and I heard the voice of many angels round about the throne and the beasts and the elders: and the number of them was ten thousand times ten thousand, and thousands of thousands; saying with a loud voice, Worthy is the Lamb that was slain to receive power, and riches, and wisdom, and strength, and honour, and glory, and blessing. And every creature which is in heaven, and on the earth, and under the earth, and such as are in the sea, and all that are in them, heard I saying, Blessing, and honour, and glory, and power, be unto him that sitteth upon the throne, and unto the Lamb for ever and ever.

Probably we've already experienced too much polemics and formal hairsplitting from professional theologians, but surely adding another voice to that mighty chorus will not be unwelcome. The author offers this book in that sense.

If the book also engages in some shortfall theologizing, it

does so mainly to create the setting for the confession. Such an approach also seems warranted in order to demonstrate the inadequacies of mere theologizing on the subject. I confess to some negative feelings about what theologians have sometimes done to truth by their attempts to dissect and categorize it.

The devil and a friend, it is said, were walking along a city street when they observed a man ahead of them going through some peculiar motions. At intervals he would stop, gaze up into the air with an ecstatic look on his face, eagerly grasp something out of the air, and clasp it to himself. The friend turned to the devil and said, "Did you see that?"

"Yes, I saw it," the devil replied.

"Doesn't that alarm you?"

"No, I'm not worried."

"I don't understand you. That man is getting hold of living truth, and that doesn't worry you? It could destroy you."

"Yes," the devil responded, "I know what living truth could do to me, but I'm not worried. You see, I know that man. He will take that living truth home, dissect it, put it in a bottle and preserve it, and then store it away on a shelf. By that time it will be quite dead."

The man was undoubtedly a professional theologian. But, of course, many theologians are also individuals of deep faith. They will not resent another voice joining the grand chorus of praise.

Whenever an author writes a book, one of the first things he must decide on is his audience. If he speaks primarily to one group, he may lose another—or at least not be taken seriously by it—and vice versa. We are all more or less prisoners of our own roles, private experiences, and language, and unless someone speaks to us within the boundaries of our individual, conceptual confinement, we may not appreciate or comprehend what he says, and lose interest.

This book attempts to appeal to a fairly broad spectrum of readers. I have not written it primarily for professionals, though some of them may find its perspective worthy of their notice. It expresses a serious point of view. The author expects that when this is realized there may be a measure of feedback from some of his theological colleagues.

Mainly it is written for those thoughtful, reasonably well-educated individuals whose roots are well established in the Bible and the Christian faith, but perhaps not in too much of its theologizing. (It is possible that one with a nonreligious or atheistic background would not really grasp the book's point of view. But then he might. It would be interesting to see whether the gospel, or even theologizing, using the method of the Master, would appeal to such persons. Surely God intended the gospel to meet the needs that all men have—even atheists. Conceivably they might be attracted by the frankly historical sections of the book. Hopefully they might also feel their hearts strangely warmed at the end.)

As to dependence, every author has his sources. I have attempted to give credit to all those I have known to be my mentors. But, of course, we can never remember every one who has influenced us. I can only hope that should any of those I have forgotten happen to read the book, they will perceive in the fact that my unconscious indebtedness to them shows through as they are given their due.

The author gratefully thanks the administrators of Loma Linda University for time off from teaching to write this volume and some other things. I also express my gratitude to all the people who have offered helpful criticisms and suggestions, especially to Cecelia St. Clair, who not only willingly endured the drudgery of the typing and retyping of the manuscript but out of her own considerable theological insight made helpful comments and recommendations. I must thank my long-suffering physician wife, who has endured enough of the author's preoccupation and seeming indifference to her needs to qualify her for the sainthood she richly deserves. As a sounding board for ideas she has been invaluable—so have been the members of my Sabbath school class, who week after week over the years have provided the conceptual probing ground where these ideas have taken shape. The author has learned much from them and from his students at the university. But above all he is grateful to the Father of us all for having given us so true a vision of Himself in His Son, and thus assuring us that we who have been so far away truly *can* go home again.

Grant   Humidifier
dad
Toyota
Uhl seals
Lock
Kevin/Angie
Wentz

6 12   Eu 3
6-27   "   1

7-4   Eu 3
8   Eu 1
9   Bf 1
9 & 10   UQC
    Rude 1

HISTORICAL DATA

Date	Time	pH	pCO₂	pO₂	tHb	sO₂	Flow	Mode	RespRt	PEEP	Vt
07/10/2003	00:39	7.506 ↑	45.8 ↑	385.2 ↑	11.3 ↓	99.8 ↑					

sO₂	99.8 ↑	%	92.0	-	98.5
O₂Hb	99.3 ↑	%	94.0	-	97.0
COHb	0.0 ↓	%	0.5	-	1.5
MetHb	0.5	%	0.0	-	1.5

LEGEND
↑ Value above reference range   ↑↑ Value above action range   ---- ↑↑ Above reporting range
↓ Value below reference range   ↓↓ Value below action range   ---- ↓↓ Below reporting range

FIO2 100%
VT 706
RR 12

P intubation ABG

Signature: _____

PATIENT REPORT

Hemet Valley Medical Center
1117 East Devonshire Avenue
Hemet, California 92543
Stephen Westbrook M.D. Medical Director

Last Name	First Name		Patient ID	Sex	Date	Time
			200996		**07/10/2003**	**00:39**

Accession No.	Operator ID				Date of Birth	

Source	Flow	Mode	RespRt	CPAP	PEEP	Vt
Arterial						
PSV - IPAP	Supplemental O2		Site			Allens Test

BLOOD GAS 37.0°C

Parameter	Value	Units	Reference Range
pH	7.506 →		7.350 - 7.450
pCO_2	45.8 →	mmHg	35.0 - 45.0
pO_2	385.2 →	mmHg	75.0 - 100.0
BP	717	mmHg	-
HCO_3^- act	35.4	mmol/L	-
BEvt	11.1	mmol/L	-

OXYGEN STATUS

Parameter	Value	Units	Reference Range
$ctO_2(a)$	16.8	mL/dL	15.0 - 23.0
$AaDO_2$	239.0	mmHg	-

OXYGENATION PARAMETERS

VE

6 – 11   m v ești
6 – 13   S 1
6 – 14   0 ești 1,2,3
   14   S 1
   25   S 1
   20   ești 1
         S 1

   26   v ești 1

   27   S 1
   28   S 1   6/21 ești 1

 3   S 1
 5   S 1
 7   S 1
 8   A 1
     ești 1
 9   E 1   3
     R 1

CHAPTER 1
Hostile or Friendly?

Throughout his existence man has continually asked three questions: Where did I come from? Why am I here? Where am I going? Individual, personal questions, they address our origin, meaning, and destiny. They relate to me and my existence. Of course, they can be asked from the standpoint of a corporate "me." Where did *we* come from? Why are *we* here? and Where are *we* going? But even in this form they remain directed at the self (selves) and its (their) place in the scheme of things.

When we shift the focus to the larger ground from which such questions emerge, they change. Instead of now asking about ourselves, we inquire about *being* itself—about the nature and meaning of reality. The three elemental questions then become: Why is there something and not nothing (the ontological question)? Is that *something* at its essential center personal or impersonal? And finally, Is that something (or someone) hostile or friendly (or neutral)? The last possibility depends, by definition, upon the answer to the second question. The word *personal,* as used here, refers to the capacity for intelligent interaction in a manner that largely excludes strict neutrality.

The first fundamental question should not detain us for long if for no other reason than that we cannot really answer it. (It is not unrelated to that childhood question your mother couldn't answer—Where did God come from?) It is unnecessary to ask it in any case. Existence is self-evident. Things are! I am, you are, and we are surrounded by a vast sea of things thrusting itself into our collective consciousness at every hand.

But the second question is a different matter. It involves the issue of whether we are alone in the cosmos. It is not just the question, however, that tantalizes so many people today in so many walks of life—from the cowboy in the ballad who wondered "at night while lying alone, if every bright star way up yonder is a big, peopled world like our own" to the space scientist who probes for the presence of life on each new planetary frontier and sends cryptic messages and signals for any mysterious civilizations that might exist in space. No, the issue is far more than just "Do we have neighbors out there?"

It has always been easy to assume that we are not alone in the universe in that sense. Remember those Martian canals, that Wellsian 1938 Martian invasion, UFOs, Flash Gordon, Buck Rogers, Star Trek, and now Luke Skywalker and *Star Wars?* Astronomers estimate that our island galaxy may contain at least 100 million planets equivalent to our own. That's easy to believe, though candor compels us to admit that, in terms of evidence that would pass muster at the Johnson Space Center in Houston, we don't have a shred to date that suggests intelligent life on any of them—even on those in our immediate solar neighborhood. All the scientific evidence, sparse as it is, leaves us utterly alone.

Most of us will probably continue to believe, however, in spite of it. We probably need to. But still this is not *the* question. The question is much more basic than peopled worlds. It is a question concerning reality itself.

When we have peeled off the vast surface layers of things—the particles, the objects, the systems, the galaxies, the quasars, and the black holes of our universe—to uncover what philosophers call the very ground of existence itself, we wonder, Is that ground personal or impersonal? It is *the* question of God. Does one spell ultimate reality *what?* or *who?*

Most thoughtful men—even the most skeptical among them—often stand in awe at the mysteries and majesties of our universe. For many of them, the wonder it inspires verges on worship. But it is the worship of "god"—beautiful, awe-inspiring, but impersonal. It is not *God.* Mainly the universe just lies there—not immobile or static, to be sure, but unaware, noninteracting, thoughtless, uncaring—a massive, roiling, impersonal, complex *thing. The* question is, Is there above, behind, and undergirding it all as its author and sustainer *Someone* who knows and cares?

The message of faith says that there is. The evidence is not empirically unequivocal, to be sure, but at least credible. It arises from the sometimes subtle, personal assurances that all men of faith understand. But more than that, it also rests on events in history, the prophecy-fulfilling kind as well as those miracle events that startle and cause wonderment. And, above all, it has its basis in the central event in history whereby One appeared who gave us out of His own intensive personality man's most transparent window on a personal Reality who knows, understands, and acts accordingly—which is what *person* means. If Jesus was what He claimed to be, then Ultimate Reality—God—is intensely personal.

The argument largely hinges, then, on who Jesus was. This book does not seek to explore the nature of that issue. Fulfilled prophecy, the authority of His life, His resurrection, and what followed in the acts and power of those who knew Him best amply support it. Belief in Jesus will always involve a committal of faith, but that does not mean an irrational leap in spite of the evidence. Men of faith find the objective evidence persuasive even if not compelling. That Jesus as the Christ is the Son of the Living God, of whom He is the normative revelation, will always involve more than mere intellectual conviction. Its claims are also moral, "heart" claims. We will return to this issue later, but since this book begins from within faith, we will at this point simply assume the answer to this second question.

The third question, however, is the one that even believers apparently have not always answered with one voice. Is Ultimate Reality hostile or friendly? This question may not always be apparent even to persons of faith. But it is hoped that both the question and the answer may unfold together in the pages that follow. In this preliminary section we shall merely try to clear away the overlying superficial debris.

The universe does, in many ways, appear hostile, at least for man. Human beings can exist only within narrow physical bounds, and stepping outside of those confines can be a most dangerous business indeed. Almost every other place in the universe that we know of is too cold, too hot, too devoid of oxygen or water, too exposed to toxic gases, radiation, or whatever, for *any* kind of life as we know it to exist—let alone human life.

The astronauts could survive on the moon, for example, only because they carried their self-contained friendly environment with them. And when one contemplates the larger whole—the fearsome distances, the awesome displays of power, the exploding suns, the black holes sucking in even light, the electronic hurricanes of unimaginable intensity—it boggles the mind!

How can one even think of the unvierse as a friendly place when so much of it ought to and does strike stark terror in the heart of so earthbound a creature? Practically all of it would be utterly devastating to the life of man were he to face it on its own terms. Thankful he may feel for the comforts of his little earthly cocoon, which has the right amount of minerals in its soil and oxygen and nitrogen in its atmosphere, the correct

HOSTILE OR FRIENDLY?

temperature, adequate water—and even the fact that water begins to expand again as it cools below 40° Fahrenheit so that it freezes at the surface instead of at the bottom. (Otherwise it would never thaw—and we would all freeze to death.) The surface of our earth is a truly marvelous conjunction of happy events and qualities—but outside of that cocoon . . . !

But even within the cocoon there is much to fear and dread. How can one speak of "friendly" in relation to the terror that stalks our city streets, that pollutes our sky and water, that hurls masses of humanity at one another's throats as they fashion ever more powerful weapons of mutual destruction, terror that leaves whole populations hungry for the ordinary requirements of sustenance, let alone the amenities, and blots out their sun with disease and private misery? The question is real and persistent. It will not simply go away.

We can readily dispose of some of the reasons for thinking of reality as hostile—that astronautical universe. Quite simply, they arise from a misconception. There is nothing instrinsically hostile about a universe in process. Those exploding suns and galaxies, the black holes, searing radiation, incredible temperature differences, wide variations in the distribution of substances, and vast distances are dangerous only to what is out of place in them—including man. In themselves they possess their own orderliness and design—just as man has his. The destructiveness that does, and should, strike terror in man's heart appears only when he leaves his appropriate niche in the scheme of things. A thing is what it is and not something else. A man is not a piece of moon rock or Martian ice—or a god! The normal operation of a dynamic natural system may be an alien environment only for a species not designed for survival in it.

This fact also has moral overtones and thus applies to that

other reason for positing hostility—man's own social and natural environment. Terror stalks those city streets and sets nation against nation simply because man has come to act against his own true nature. The moral law, insofar as it reflects reality rather than a perversion or misperception of it, describes that actuality.

For example, that Old Testament moral code, the Ten Commandments—while admittedly a time-place expression of what morality is about—nonetheless accurately describes what it takes to keep human life human. To illustrate, the first part of the Decalogue highlights the fact that man achieves his true importance in committal to something (in the specific terms of the Ten Commandments, Some*one*) greater than himself. And a way to achieve such fulfillment is through an appropriate expression of that fact. The Sabbath is a celebration of creatureliness in its proper posture toward the Creator.

Man was made for community—he is a social being. No community can exist apart from trust—keeping one's word and living up to one's contracts. Therefore, man, when true to himself, does not bear false witness. Community also involves respect for one's neighbor and the things that pertain to him—and especially for his life.

Man was made for social continuity. Community calls for respect of one generation for another. "Honour thy father and thy mother." The continuity also includes the integrity of the more intimate community—the family—and so we have the seventh commandment. One could write an entire book on such matters, but the point is, when true to himself (and these moral maxims portray that self) man fulfills himself. Social hostility results when man violates the integrity of his being.

Breaking the commandments is not so much an affront to

God—although it does do that also—as it is a violating of one's own being. Moral rules, as surely as the laws of the larger natural universe, become hostile only when humanity defies them. One cannot ignore or flaunt the laws of his being with impunity.

We shall want to explore this concept more fully, since it forms the backdrop for another kind of misperception. Existing even in the minds of people who should know better, it has to do with whether *God* is friendly or hostile toward those who have defied His laws. Does a person who runs into the menacing consequences of those laws he has spurned also confront an angry God in that defiance? It seems logical enough that one should, and plenty of guilt-ridden, fearful individuals have thought so. The Scriptures abound with references to the wrath of God, His fierce anger, et cetera. And there is in most of us enough cryptic childhood memory of parental anger to provide the subconscious soil for such a noxious, conceptual weed cover. Guilt—real or false, or even neurotic—almost demands it. But is it so? The New Testament tells of Him who loved us "while we were yet sinners" (Rom. 5:8). It portrays the human face of God, who out of love (John 3:16) came not "into the world to condemn the world" (verse 17).

Some of the dominant historic concepts of our Lord's saving acts rest on an implicit concept of divine outrage. And that's what this book is about.

Let us begin by asking the question in a slightly different way. In changing its form we may seem to have diverted our attention slightly, but hopefully the direction we are taking will gradually become apparent.

CHAPTER 2

The Crucial Question

It is ironic that the question whether God is essentially friendly or hostile should have been raised historically at the very center of the good news (gospel).

Andrew Lloyd Webber and Tim Rice, in their outrageous *Jesus Christ, Superstar,* pose the question in the mouth of Jesus Himself. But their depiction of Jesus as Himself asking that question distorts the story almost to the point of sacrilege. Actually, Jesus seemed to have little question about why He must die. To be sure, He was not eager for it. In Gethsemane His sensitive soul recoiled in horror at the prospect. But He well understood why He had to go through with it. His humanness was apparently unable to preview entirely its final agony and a Why? was finally wrung from His anguished lips, but even then He did not question the act so much as its terrifying aloneness. He apparently had not anticipated that.

The question "Why did He have to die?" is ours, not His. And a great deal of Christian theology during the two millenniums since then has attempted to answer it in one way or another.

The writers of the New Testament Gospels and letters were more preoccupied with the *fact* of His life, death, and what came after than they were with the *why* of it. They really did not even ask that question. Instead, they—especially the most nearly systematic theologian of the lot, Paul—provided the metaphors that would become the basis for later theological answers, but it appears that to them the event itself loomed more important than any studied analysis of it could possibly be. And, of course, they were right.

But, since we are exploring the deeper issues out of which our question arises, we cannot ignore those later theories. They do have a bearing on our present understanding. Ideas are rarely immaculately conceived—they nearly always have a past. Every present thinker who really wants to know what is going through his mind must be aware of what others have thought and expressed before.

It is not to say that current ideas merely repeat the past. That never completely happens. But it does mean that we are prisoners of the past more than we often realize. And this could include being trapped in its linguistic forms.

One of the difficulties we experience in tracing the history of ideas has to do with the language in which they are expressed. Merely to repeat the verbal formulas does not guarantee a continuity of thought. For example, all of the theologians used Scripture to support their theoretical constructs. By doing so they seemed to imply that they were simply adopting Biblical thought patterns. But what the Biblical writer may have originally intended as a useful, momentary metaphor—designed to enlighten a particular aspect of truth—we sometimes pushed in this way to a literal absurdity.

And, of course, that is one of the difficulties we encounter as we seek to interpret the Bible properly. It deals with ideas larger than language. And how does one speak the unspeakable? One way is to translate the "Word" into "flesh" (as in John 1:14), that is, to paint a picture—verbal or otherwise. Symbols, figures of speech, metaphors—even metaphorical stories, or parables—are the Biblical writers' brushes and tubes of paint.

Part of the reason Jesus spoke in parables was to ensure that His messages would not become locked into the strictures of specific time and place. What He had to say was timeless and for every place, and so He told stories that could belong to all of us wherever and whenever we should live.

But we can never take eternal ideas compressed into time at literal face value in every aspect. We must be "carried beyond" the literal words (which is what *metaphor* means). And that was the main trouble with those theories about why Jesus had to die. The theologians pushed Biblical metaphor further than figures of speech were ever intended to go, that is, if we take the theories literally. (Sometimes we can't be sure. Occasionally the theologian gives a hint that he may be speaking with tongue in cheek. Unfortunately, too often he seems to intend that we should take what he's propounding in concrete literal terms—even if at this distance that may seem quite incredible.)

In the following pages we shall simply assume that the representative theologian is speaking in a straightforward manner. (Unfortunately this may be unfair to a particular theologian who may have said other things in other contexts that might give a quite different balance to his pronouncements. We must remember that even theologians are rarely as simple as they may appear on occasion.)

Selections made in such an arbitrary manner are bound to be inaccurate in some respects. Perhaps we can mitigate the situation somewhat by stating that what we intend here is not to categorize the thoughts of specific theologians so much as to sketch certain dominant ideas which various ones seem to have supported by some of the things they said. (At the same time we recognize that the general direction of their thought might in fact have been quite otherwise.) In other words, we are caricaturing ideas rather than characterizing persons.

One thing more we must add before we proceed. About those ideas that have a past, they also have a present; that is, they reflect the experiential contexts in which we express them, especially where we employ metaphor. Speech figures cannot carry beyond if they do not begin where we are. What this means in terms of our present interest is that we must remember that those theories about why Jesus had to die necessarily reflect and represent a part of the fabric of the society and times that formulated them. For example, the notion of Jesus ransoming us from Satan gained significance from the North African pirates who in those days preyed on Mediterranean shipping and held important citizens for payment.

Thus it was not simply a question of rhetorical utility. Theologians were not merely drawing on convenient illustrations. Rather, what they did was inevitable because of the way the human mind works. All understanding or awareness occurs in terms of our previous perception of experience. New experiences filter through the kind of people we are, what we have done, and what we have thought. In the process they take on the characteristics of the filter. In other words, we see things not as *they* are, but in terms of what *we* are. Ideas, then, even our own ideas, have a history in us that parallels or own history. What we have been, what we are, and what we will become reflect themselves in how we look at things. (And here is one of the difficulties we face as we try to capture a theologian's perspective. We always have to ask ourselves, At what particular time in his life and development did he say that? Some have said of the modern theologian Karl Barth that his was theology always "on the wing." But that's more or less true of all thinkers insofar as they are creative.)

It is also the case that how we perceive things may project a certain amount of need, and wish fulfillment. The ransom notion, at least for some who held it, was probably not just an illustration. It provided a conceptual model that enabled its proponents to avoid personal responsibility for what happened to them and thus released them from overt guilt over their own personal failure. Such a concept took things out of their hands and placed them in the divine marketplace.

We must continually keep this point in mind in what follows. Also it should caution us from making any point in history or any particular concept normative for all time. As transcendent a truth as that about God may continue to unfold for eternity—and maybe that's what heaven is for. Of one thing we can be certain—whatever was said in the past, be the spokesman prophet or theologian (and there *is* a difference), even things stated in this book, we must never take them to be the final word. All that we can hope for is that we can learn to stay on the proper path as we journey along—and at least avoid some of the pitfalls into which even honest and wise men have sometimes fallen.

But first let us look at some of the ways men have answered the question regarding the meaning of Christ's death, at the same time remembering that as we ask this question, we are also asking the deeper one, ("Is God hostile or friendly?")

CHAPTER 3

Is "Free" a Bargain?

The writings of the early Church Fathers (whose work generally predates theology in a classical sense) largely repeated the apostles' attitude toward the cross and its meaning. The event itself simply overshadowed any possible explanations. Therefore, they struggled for adequate metaphors to describe it. But two statements of Jesus and a number of Pauline passages gradually became the basis for a motif that remained dominant down to the eighth century and in a modified form until the time of Anselm (A.D. 1033-1109).

Jesus had said that He had come to give His life a ransom for many (Matt. 20:28; Mark 10:45). Paul referred to "redemption" in a number of familiar passages, to "bondage" and to "liberty" in Christ (for example, Gal. 5:1). In 1 Corinthians 7:23 he said, "Ye are bought with a price." Such passages suggested some kind of transaction or bargain with the enemy. While the early Church Fathers also employed other metaphors, including the legal language so strong in Paul's letter to the Romans, the bargaining notion appears most often in their writings whenever they speculated on the subject—which was apparently not often. Redemption remained, for most of them at least, theoretically an experience and not a doctrine.

In its crudest essentials the ransom theory suggested that when man fell from grace he became the devil's possession and, however it came about, a just God could not ignore it. In order to free man from this bondage, He agreed to pay a price, the death of His own Son. Since the Son's value was more than that of all the damned souls together, Satan willingly entered into the arrangement. But, alas, in accepting the payment he was deceived. Satan, unable to hold the Son of God in his power, thus lost both the souls of the damned and the soul of the Son of God.

Origen (A.D. 185-254) stated the terms of the bargain:

> If then we were "bought with a price," as also Paul asserts, we were doubtless bought from one whose servants we were, who also named what price he would for releasing those whom he held from his power. Now it was the devil that held us, to whose side we had been drawn away by our sins. He asked, therefore, as our price the blood of Christ. . . . For he held us until the ransom for us, even the soul of Jesus, was paid to him, being deceived into thinking that he could be its lord, and not seeing that he could not bear the torment of holding it.[1]

A century later Gregory of Nyssa gave us the classical expression of the theory, adding a twist of his own to the story that would appear in one form or another again and again. Even Martin Luther used it.

> In order to secure that the ransom in our behalf might be easily accepted by him who required it, the Deity was hidden under the veil of our nature, that so, as with ravenous fish, the hook of the Deity might be gulped down along with the bait of flesh.[2]

God's deception of the devil in the transaction apparently didn't disturb Origen. Others were. Gregory of Nyssa, for example, consoled himself that the "deceiver" (Satan) deserved it. But the moral implications of God's deception were unlikely to be too pressing in a world where Christians condoned falsehood if it supported God's honor and where they felt in unnecessary to keep faith with heretics. Most of them considered the clever trick as a mark of God's sagacity.

The hook-bait metaphor appears in the writings of a number of authors during this period. Rufinus even found a text for it. Job 41:1 says, "Canst thou draw out leviathan with an hook?"

The metaphor also took other forms. Gregory the Great used the hook-bait motif, but also referred to the cross as a snare for catching birds. "The Lord deceived him like a bird when in the Passion He displayed before him His only begotten Son as bait, but hid the noose."[3] Augustine compared the cross to a mousetrap. "As our price He held out His cross to him like a mousetrap, and as bait set upon it His own blood."[4] These great writers knew they were employing figures of speech, of course. Mainly they wished to emphasize that the devil was a fool.

Some of them wondered whether the devil really had any just claim upon sinners, since he had captured them in the first place by deception. But generally the writers assumed that whatever its legal status, God had demonstrated His own superior justice by treating the claim as valid. He conquered Satan with justice and righteousness rather than with might.

The fact that so crude a motif as the transaction theory of the atonement would continue to surface for nearly a thousand years seems proof positive of how little speculative theology was directed during that period to why Christ had to die. It was a convenient explanation, appropriate to the intellectual climate of the day, and easily adapted to homiletic purposes. (Actually, it may have been of little more importance than that. In any case, one doubts that it really often expressed the deeper thoughts of those who used it.) To us today it is mainly important because the notion of a transaction forms the conceptual base for the later objective atonement theories that theology did take much more seriously.

Other ways of thinking about Christ's death appeared from time to time. During the third and fourth centuries mystical concepts surfaced in several of the early Fathers, mainly in the Eastern part of Christendom. The essence of the notion involved man's mystical identity with God. Paul had laid the groundwork for it in such statements as those found in Romans 6, where he states that the follower of Christ is crucified with Christ and buried and raised with Him. Since we are one with Him, in His death *we* die for our sins and in His victory *we* gain the victory over Satan. What He achieves, we all mystically achieve. Irenaeus presented the idea in a slightly different form, in what some have called a recapitulation view of Christ's life and death. According to him, mankind in its solidarity is bound together in Christ's victory, just as it fell collectively in Adam.

Even Gregory of Nyssa—who extolled God's outwitting of the devil—apparently also grasped the mystical possibility whereby the life of Christ becomes our life. In such authors we also begin to see hints of ideas that would become the dominant motifs of the later, more explicitly theological period.

Western Latin Christianity typically had a more practical bent than did the Hellenic East. As a consequence it is almost exclusively in the West that thoroughgoing doctrines concerning why Christ had to die developed. Profoundly influenced by the legalisms of the great Roman system of jurisprudence, its interests were more ethical than mystical. None captured the mood of the West more surely than the first of the great theologians to come to grips with the death of Christ in a systematic theological way, Saint Anselm of Canterbury.

---

[1] Quoted in L. W. Grensted, *A Short History of the Doctrine of the Atonement* (London: Butler & Tanner, Ltd., 1920), pp. 37, 38.
[2] *Ibid.*, p. 40.
[3] *Ibid.*, p. 44.
[4] *Ibid.*

CHAPTER 4

Cur Deus Homo?

It is almost impossible to overestimate the influence of Anselm of Canterbury on the development of modern speculation regarding the purpose of Christ's death. Some have said that he virtually created the doctrine of the atonement. Certainly he put an end to earlier transactional thinking. No one in the preceding centuries had brought such systematic, critical, almost scientific (there was no real science yet) analysis to the subject as appeared in *Cur Deus Homo?* ("Why Did God Become Man?").

Like almost everybody else in his day, he showed a deep dependence on the great Augustine, of the fourth and fifth centuries. (Augustine himself, while deeply perceptive, never presented a consistent atonement theory. But he did lay the ground for later systematics.) Both Augustine (354-430) and his later pupil Gregory the Great (540(?)-604) had suggested that there existed something in the very essence of God's own nature, some quality of absolute justice perhaps, that demanded Christ's death for our sins. Neither had developed the idea, however. Both conceived of God in some ways as a Roman judge administering law. Also, both saw the difficulty presented to justice by what they felt to be His releasing of the guilty and punishment of the innocent.

Anselm understood this question well. In *Cur Deus Homo?* he had his character Bozo ask in their extended conversation:

> For what justice is there in giving up the most just man of all to death on behalf of the sinner? What man would not be judged worthy of condemnation if he condemned the innocent in order to free the guilty? . . . For if he could not save sinners except by condemning the just, where is his omnipotence? But if he could, but would not, how are we to defend his wisdom and justice?[1]

Anselm attempted at length to solve the difficulty.

The world had changed mightily by the eleventh century, when Anselm came along, including the political system. The Roman Empire had given way to the feudal system, where the figure of the feudal lord, surrounded by his serfs, provided the characteristic social unit. Roman law thus became highly personalized in this context. Law and justice were personal matters. Lawbreaking was conceived as a direct offense against a person—mainly *the* person, the feudal lord who epitomized the contemporary social structure.

Among the principles of Roman law still current was the notion that one could provide satisfaction as an alternative to punishment in the case of private offenses. However, if the offender did not give satisfaction, the offense must be punished. This principle had long conditioned the penitential system of the Roman Church. The church concluded that one might offer penance to God in the present life as an alternative to eternal death, which was the proper punishment for sin in the world to come. By thus providing satisfaction, the penalty could be paid.

Anselm's satisfaction theory was the logical expression of such a social milieu. For Anselm, God was virtually a cosmic equivalent of the feudal lord. Anselm defined sin as dishonoring God in much the same way that a feudal serf might dishonor his lord on an earthly scale. "To sin is the same thing as not to render his due to God," he stated in *Cur Deus Homo?* We owe Him the subjection of our will to the divine will in all things so that we might preserve righteousness. "One who does not render this honour to God takes away from God what belongs to him, and dishonours God, and to do this is to sin."[2]

And in rectifying the situation, Anselm said:

And it is not enough merely to return what was taken away; in

> view of the insult committed, he must give back more than he took away.... It is not enough for someone who violates another's honour to restore the honour, unless he makes some kind of restitution that will please him who was dishonoured, according to the extent of the injury and dishonour.... So, then, everyone who sins must repay to God the honour that he has taken away, and this is the satisfaction that every sinner ought to make to God.[3]

(The last phrase is the basis for labeling Anselm's theory the satisfaction theory.)

For God to demand less would strike at order itself.

> Nothing is less tolerable in the order of things, than for the creature to take away the honour due to the Creator and not repay what he takes away.... Therefore, either the honour that was taken away must be repaid or punishment must follow. Otherwise, God will be either unjust to himself or powerless to accomplish either; but it is impious even to imagine this.[4]

The central theme of Anselm's thesis was that God, the cosmic feudal overlord, must safeguard His honor and demand either punishment or adequate satisfaction as a vindication of His outraged dignity. He cannot tolerate having His personal honor violated without such vindication.

Anselm repeated Augustine's argument that God must save at least some men to fill the vacancies left by fallen angels. If it were not for that fact, He could be content with merely punishing them. Unfortunately, because of the enormity of sin, that would result in the death of all sinners. God therefore had to proceed by the only way open to Him, the way of satisfaction.

Man is himself unable to provide it, however. A sinner cannot justify a sinner.[5] Sin's enormity requires that it come from

Someone "greater than everything that exists, except God. . . . Then no one but God can make this satisfaction."[6]

But since man owes the debt, he must also pay it. Therefore, only a God-man can provide the satisfaction. God because only He can do it. Man because only he owes it.[7] The God-man is our incarnate Lord, the Son of God, who is also the Son of man. For Anselm, that's why Jesus had to die.

Anselm did not really come into his own until the following century and afterward. One of his younger colleagues and for a time pupil, Peter Abelard (1079-1142), became famous for a quite different kind of notion about why Christ had to die, somewhat erroneously called the moral influence theory. Abelard saw the death of Christ as unnecessary as far as it concerned God's forgiveness. God had been able to forgive before Christ's death and could continue to forgive whomever He chose. For Abelard the death of Christ remained primarily a profound demonstration of God's love designed to awaken a love response in us.

He wrote in his commentary on Romans:

> We have been justified by the blood of Christ and reconciled to God in this way; through this unique act of grace manifested to us—in that his Son has taken upon himself our nature and preserved therein in teaching us by word and example even unto death—he has more fully bound us to himself by love; with the result that our hearts should be enkindled by such a gift of divine grace, and true charity should not now shrink from enduring anything for him. . . . Yet everyone becomes more righteous—by which we mean a greater lover of the Lord—after the Passion of Christ than before, since a realized gift inspires greater love than one which is only hoped for. Wherefore, our redemption through Christ's suffering is that deeper affection in us which not only frees

us from slavery to sin, but also wins for us the true liberty of sons of God, so that we do all things out of love rather than fear.[8]

Unfortunately, the church excommunicated Peter Abelard (mainly on other grounds than this teaching, however) and his real influence on atonement theology would not be felt until many centuries later.

After Anselm, Western theology largely divided into two schools of thought, the Thomists (Thomas Aquinas 1225(?)-1274) and the Scotists (John Duns Scotus—1265(?)-1308), who while differing markedly on other matters, agreed that the atonement was not absolutely necessary. Thomas Aquinas said that God could simply have remitted man's sin, but by using the method of satisfaction, He was able to bestow certain other benefits, such as being able to reveal His love and give us an example that would inspire us to new freedom. Here he seems to draw on Abelard. But he is inconsistent. He also speaks of Christ's passion as "a true sacrifice"[9] offered for the purpose of placating God.[10] Yet he also shifts Anselm's satisfaction notion in the direction of the later legal, or forensic, theory, which we shall examine shortly. "In this," he wrote, "is shown the severity of God, who wills not to remit sin without punishment."[11]

The mystical concepts of Eastern Christendom also appeared in Thomas. "The voluntary suffering of Christ was so great a good that for this good found in human nature God was appeased in regard to all the offence of mankind, as far as concerns those who are joined to Christ in His suffering."[12]

Duns Scotus contested Aquinas at almost every point— except in the idea that the death of Christ was not absolutely necessary. For him Christ's sufferings had only human value and were finite in every respect. They were sufficient to make satisfaction for man's sin and then only because God chose to accept them as such.[13] "If you ask how far Christ's merit had sufficient worth, it had worth without doubt as far as it was accepted by God."[14] For Duns Scotus even an angel could have provided the satisfaction if God had wished to accept it.[15] There are, he felt, no limits to what God might accept if He chose.

---

[1] Anselm of Canterbury, *Cur Deus Homo?* The Library of Christian Classics (Philadelphia: The Westminster Press, 1956), Vol. X, p. 111. (The Reformers would have done well to have read this chapter in Cur Deus Homo?)
[2] *Ibid.*, p. 119.
[3] *Ibid.*
[4] *Ibid.*, p. 122.
[5] *Ibid.*, p. 141.
[6] *Ibid.*, pp. 150, 151.
[7] *Ibid.*, p. 152.
[8] Peter Abelard, *Exposition of the Epistle to the Romans*, The Library of Christian Classics (Philadelphia: The Westminster Press, 1956), Vol X, pp. 283, 284.
[9] Quoted in L. W. Grensted, *The Doctrine of the Atonement*, p. 154.
[10] *Ibid.*
[11] Aquinas, *Summa* III, Q. 47, quoted in Grensted.
[12] Aquinas, *Summa* III, Q. 49, quoted in Grensted. p. 155.
[13] Quoted in Grensted, p. 160.
[14] *Ibid.*
[15] *Ibid.*, p. 161.

CHAPTER 5

What Price Justice?

The period between Anselm and the Reformation produced no clear direction. Many voices competed with one another. Anselm's legal alternatives, punishment or satisfaction, never quite carried the day. Penance was a problem, as was a new sense of the divine justice. Gerson (1363-1429) said:

> God would never permit unpunished evil and therefore laid all our sins and faults upon Jesus Christ. [Well might he have read Bozo's question in *Cur Deus Homo?*] Sin is very greatly to be hated because it very greatly displeases the Divine Justice [notice, now, *justice* rather than honor], for you behold God suffering the penalty due to sin, in order to destroy it.[1]

Wycliffe (1324(?)-1384) had shown the same tendency, but he also stressed the role of penitence—indeed, to so great an extent that he virtually nullified Anselm's satisfaction theory with which his thought was otherwise generally compatible. He said:

> It is right that that man (Adam) should be saved, since he repented so fruitfully, and God cannot deny His pity to such a penitent.... There is no doubt that God cannot refuse to grant the abolition of sin to those who are fruitfully contrite.[2]

The Roman Church, meanwhile, took a contrasting direction. A major point of conflict between the Reformers and the Roman Church had to do with the concept of righteousness—what the theologians called justification and sanctification. To the major Continental Reformers, man's righteousness resulted solely by divine declaration. It was an act of God in which man did not and could not participate. At the Council of Trent (1545-1563) the Roman Church defined justification (being declared righteous) as including sanctification (being righteous).

Trent, in short, rejected the highly external quality of the Reformers' legal interpretation of God's action. It was not merely something done *for* man, it also happened *to* him; and it permitted, even if sometimes only to a small degree, human participation in the process. (One could hear occasional echoes of Abelard at Trent—love in man responds to love in God.) The Reformers by contrast stressed the worthlessness of all human effort.

While Trent theoretically placed emphasis on the grace of God, in practice the ordinary life of the church continued to stress human merits, human effort, indulgences, and the like. In theory at least, the merit ideal also included Christ's merits. The popular manual *Catholic Belief* expresses a similar thought even today.

> All our merits, however, without any exception, are grounded on the merits of Jesus Christ, and on His grace, without which no one can move a step towards heaven.... Our merit, therefore, does not take away from Christ's merits, for without Him we can do nothing. We merit through Christ, Christ makes us merit; or still more properly, Christ merits in us, and therefore all the glory is His.[3]

(Later on we shall ask whether we should question the merit concept itself, not just *whose* merits.)

In the Roman Church the idea of making restitution and satisfaction tended to shift in the direction of a human act, to a sacrifice regarded in part as an expiation of sin, but also as an act of homage and worship. The meritorious act is something one brings to God. The doctrine of the Eucharist—the mass—played no small part in this development.

Hints of a number of positions that would become settled in the minds of the Reformers appeared here and there, but mainly what took place as we approach the next period was a change in the political and intellectual atmosphere as feudalism began to wane. With this political transformation came modifications of the conception of why Christ had to die.

The more prominent Reformers did not greatly concern themselves with the atonement question. Rather they directed their energies at countering the medieval doctrine of merits, the human contribution to man's salvation. But they, nonetheless, more or less consistently came to espouse an interpretation of Christ's sacrifice that remains profoundly influential even to the present day. A revival of Roman law and especially a legal notion of justice, it represents a watershed for thinking about why Christ died.

The Reformation atonement theory goes under various names: penal, legal, forensic, sometimes governmental (although the latter introduces a slightly different thought). Forensic is probably the most common term. In many ways it depended on Anselm's satisfaction theory, but its presuppositions are sufficiently different that it qualifies for independent existence.

Hints of the forensic theory existed before the Reformation. At least some of the Reformers themselves seemed to think that they were simply restating Anselm. His formula and language appears frequently in their writings. But the political scene had changed, and the feudal principle had given place to a concept of abstract law and particularly an abstract notion of justice requiring punishment. The death of Jesus now fulfilled a legal requirement. A crime had been committed (sin) for which the just penalty was death. Justice demanded payment for the penalty, which Jesus met, since no man's life is of sufficient worth to compensate for more than his own individual crimes.

We now find no trace here of Anselm's punishment or satisfaction alternative. It is not God who requires satisfaction so much as it is abstract justice. The dictates of justice bind even God Himself. A just God can do no other. Jesus' death adequately substitutes for the requirements of justice. (Anselm's literary character Bozo would probably ask again, "For what justice is there in giving up the most just Man of all to death on behalf of the sinner?" But Bozo's question seems not to have disturbed most of the Reformers, mainly because they did not appear to realize that the forensic solution involved a legal confusion—that between civil and criminal law. Civil law permits substitute reparation. Your insurance company may make payment for your wrongful act. But criminal law demands that the perpetrator of the crime also receive the punishment for it.)

The weakness of the theory lies, of course, in its underlying retributive concept of justice—which we shall discuss later.

The first generation of Reformers—especially Martin Luther, who was a mystic more than he was a systematic theologian and often inconsistent in his pronouncements—do not give us our clearest expression of the concept. They mainly concerned themselves with combatting the excesses of the Roman merit system, indulgences, and the like—especially as expressed in a human works salvation—than they were with precise theological hairsplitting. We owe to Melanchthon (1497-1560) the most precise Reformation statement of the forensic theory of justification. He defined it as

> To justify, in accordance with forensic usage, here signified to acquit the accused and to pronounce him righteous, but on account of the righteousness of another, namely of Christ, which righteousness of another is communicated to us by faith.[4]

Melanchthon wrote in the Augsburg Confession of 1530 (the principle creed of Lutheranism and both historically and doctrinally the most important statement of the beliefs of the Reformation—the Protestant potentates signed it, though Luther said he himself "could not tread so gently and softly"):

> Also they teach that men cannot be justified [obtain forgiveness of sins and righteousness] before God by their own powers, merits, or works, but are justified freely [of grace] for Christ's sake through faith, when they believe that they are received into favor, and their sins forgiven for Christ's sake, who by his death hath satisfied for our sins. This faith doth God impute for righteousness before him.[5]

The Augsburg Confession in a phrase more pertinent to our question, Why did Christ have to die? also reoriented the Pauline "reconcile . . . unto God" (Eph. 2:16)* when it talked of

> one Christ, true God and true man; who was born of the virgin Mary, truly suffered, was crucified, dead, and buried, that he might *reconcile the Father unto us* [Italics supplied. Could they also have said "angry" Father?], and might be a sacrifice, not only for original guilt, but also for all actual sins of men.[6]

Luther said of Christ's sacrifice for sin:

> Who has and bears in His own body all the sins of all men—not in that He committed them, but in that He took upon His own body the things committed by us, to make satisfaction for them with His own blood.
>
> If the sins of the whole world are upon that one man, Jesus Christ, then are they not upon the world. . . . if Christ Himself was made guilty of all the sins which we have committed, then are we absolved from all sins, yet not through ourselves, our own works or merits, but through Him.[7]

The concept seems in keeping with Paul's statement in 2

---

* See also 2 Corinthians 5:19, 20: "To wit, that God was in Christ, reconciling the world unto himself. . . . In Christ's stead, be ye reconciled to God."

Corinthians 5:21: "For he hath made him to be sin for us, who knew no sin." But the Reformation position, at least as stated by its systematic spokesman, Melanchthon, takes us immediately into deep water as it asks why God had to do this. For Melanchthon as for many another troubled Christian—and he seems less troubled than some—the love of God is never as powerful a motif as His wrath against sin.

> God's wondrous plan is set forth, that though He is just and is horribly angry at sin, yet at last He will be willing that His most just wrath should be placated, because His Son is made a suppliant for us and has drawn down the wrath upon Him, and is made an expiation and a victim for us.[8]

Again, in his expansion of the Augsburg Confession for the Saxon churches, Melanchthon wrote:

> Such is the severity of His justice that reconciliation would not be made unless the penalty were utterly paid. Such is the greatness of His wrath that the eternal Father would not be placated save by the entreaty and death of the Son. Such is His mercy, that the Son was given for us. Such love was in the Son toward us that He drew down this true and great wrath upon Himself.[9]

"Christ's benefits are these: to bear guilt and eternal death, that is, to placate the great wrath of God."[10]

Here a subjective element on man's part creeps in:

> For the heart, truly feeling that God is angry, cannot love God, unless He is shown to be placated. While He terrifies us and seems to be casting us into eternal death, human nature cannot raise itself up to love Him that is angry, that judges and punishes.[11]

The great Calvin expressed similar sentiments. "He offered as a sacrifice the flesh he received from us, that he might wipe out our guilt by his act of expiation and appease the Father's righteous wrath." [12] "But, before we go any further, we must see in passing how fitting it was that God, who anticipates us by his mercy, should have been our enemy *until he was reconciled to us through Christ.*" (Italics supplied.)[13]

Calvin apparently did not intend to convey the stark literalism that it was all too easy for some of his followers to read into his words, for he immediately qualifies himself:

> Expressions of this sort hve been accommodated to our capacity that we may better understand how miserable and ruinous our condition is apart from Christ. For if it had not been clearly stated that the wrath and vengeance of God and eternal death rested upon us, we would scarcely have recognized how miserable we would have been without God's mercy, and we would have underestimated the benefit of liberation.[14]

To speak of it as an accommodation, however, does not mean that we should ignore the language regarding God's wrath. It corresponds to something essential in God's character.

> Although this statement is tempered to our feeble comprehension, it is not said falsely. For God, who is the highest righteousness, cannot love the unrighteousness that he sees in us all. All of us, therefore, have in ourselves something deserving of God's hatred. . . . Therefore to take away all cause for enmity and to reconcile us utterly to himself, he wipes out all evil in us by the expiation set forth in the death of Christ; that we, who were previously unclean and impure, may show ourselves righteous and holy in his sight. . . . For actually, through him alone we escape the imputation of our sins to us—an imputation bringing with it the wrath of God.[15]

We should note that for both Calvin an Melanchthon, God's hatred is directed at the sin and not necessarily at the sinner, although when the reference is to unrighteousness in us the distinction will likely seem somewhat academic. We are so identified with our sin that it is scarcely possible in practice to fail to see God's wrath aimed at us.

Most important for our interest, Calvin's answer to the question "Why did Christ have to die?" contains the thought that our sin has outraged God's avenging justice. And in order to allow love to operate, there must be a full satisfying of its claims. The way to accomplish that is to transfer God's vengeance to His Son, which is to say Jesus died to meet the demands of God's justice so that His forgiving love could express itself toward the sinner.

> This is our acquittal: the guilt that held us liable for punishment has been transferred to the head of the Son of God [Isa. 53:12]. We must, above all, remember this substitution, lest we tremble and remain anxious throughout life—as if God's righteous vengeance, which the Son of God has taken upon himself, still hung over us.[16]

Unfortunately, another statement by Calvin suggests that the whole thing is a legal fiction. If Christ really bore our guilt, then God should also have directed His just hostility toward Him, but we read, "Yet we do not suggest that God was ever inimical or angry toward him. How could he be angry toward his beloved Son?" Instead Christ "bore the weight of divine severity . . . and experienced all the *signs* of a wrathful and avenging God."[17] (Italics supplied.) Apparently God acted toward Him only *as though* He were angry.

Nagging difficulties remain. Anselm's confusion of civil and criminal law still persists as does Bozo's unanswered question.

While Calvin and others like him spoke of God's offended justice as demanding punishment, they were, in fact, expressing an abstract concept of retribution that could also operate apart from God. Justice demands its due. For every crime there must be a punishment that suits the crime—or injustice results. Forgiveness without penalty would be unjust—hence Jesus' death as a substitute. Somebody had to pay! (We shall return to this in a moment.)

After Calvin, minor modifications in the position of the early Reformers occurred—generally in the direction of formal accuracy. The main principles enunciated by Luther and Calvin changed little in principle. Some would ask about man's part in the process. Osiander (1498-1552) would return to the Roman position that God's saving act *made* righteous rather than merely *imputing* righteousness.

Some of the divines would tend to forget Calvin's statement that God was not angry with His Son. The Heidelberg Catechism (1563) explicitly stated that Christ endured the divine wrath. Also many reverted to the mystical identity with Christ that made His death effective in our behalf.

The English Reformation quickly took a position not too different from that of the Roman Church. Bishop Cranmer, for example, was not far from Aquinas in his concept of the value of human good works. An increasing Calvinism in England, however, soon overshadowed this, and the later Hooker would strongly oppose the Roman doctrine of merits. Most Anglican divines warned against dogmatizing too much on "so mysterious a subject." Butler warned against going beyond Scripture.

The Socinians of Poland criticized the Reformers' penal concepts—especially the satisfaction notion. For them God's freedom permitted God to do whatever He willed—even remitting satisfaction altogether if He wished. Thus they tended to underrate both the seriousness of evil and the holiness of God. They also asked Bozo's question, about how an unjust act such as

Christ's murder could satisfy justice, in ways that made Calvinists squirm. In the process, the Socinians virtually abandoned the atonement idea.

The changing political scene altered the penal theory of why Christ had to die more than did any Socinian criticism. Gradually it became apparent that the integrity of the state depended more on an orderly, settled government than upon the arbitrary supremacy of an individual ruler. Under the influence of Hugo Grotius (1583-1645), who had been a lawyer, the new political developments led to what was, in fact, a new theory of why Christ had to die (even if Grotius thought he was defending orthodox Calvinism. For him, Christ's death was not so much a satisfaction of abstract justice as an assertion of it.) Punishment for sin, the new concept held, seeks to preserve the social order of the universe.

We find here a subtle but fairly radical shift in man's conception of God. He acts not in terms of His own sovereign will, but to preserve something He values—an orderly universe. (The theory later became known as the governmental or rectoral theory.)

Grotius wholeheartedly accepted the substitutional aspect of the penal theory, but again failed to answer Bozo's question—even though he tried by giving examples from the Old Testament and Roman and pagan history. Justice for Grotius was administrative justice designed to deter crime and to restore order. It had no absolute role in the scheme of things. Its strict demands might even be relaxed so long as good government is obtained. (Actually this notion is not far from the essence of Abelard's moral-influence theory—only that for Grotius, Christ's death acts as a vicarious deterrent to sin rather than a winsome expression of love.)

Grotius received criticism—and rightly so, mainly by John

Crell—for failing to justify the punishment of an innocent person and for not distinguishing between civil and criminal law, both weaknesses of the theories that had preceded him.

His influence in a kind of combination with Socinianism began to shape theology outside of orthodox Calvinism. The Arminians, for example, developed a modified form of the rectoral theory. Wesleyan theologians took the notion over almost in its entirety (even though it does not appear in John Wesley's writings. Apparently Wesley, himself, held to a modified satisfaction concept.)

Multiplication and diversity of theories have characterized the modern period. Few contemporaries hold rigidly to the old theories. Still almost all of them persist in one form or another except for the transaction concept. The classical penal formulation has tended to lose influence almost to the point of extinction among many prominent theologians. Abelard's moral influence concept is apparently the only one that has come to receive a more adequate expression.

---

[1] Quoted in L. W. Grensted, *The Doctrine of the Atonement*, p. 169.
[2] *Ibid*, p. 170.
[3] *Ibid*, p. 188.
[4] *Ibid*, p. 193.
[5] Philip Schaff, *The Creeds of Christendom* (New York: Harper & Brothers, 1877), Vol. III, p. 10.
[6] *Ibid*, p. 9.
[7] Quoted in Grensted, *op. cit.*, p. 200.
[8] *Ibid*, p. 206.
[9] *Ibid*.
[10] *Ibid*, p. 207.
[11] *Ibid*.
[12] John Calvin, *Institutes*, Book II, Chap. 12, par. 3.
[13] *Ibid*, chap. 16, par. 2.
[14] *Ibid*.
[15] *Ibid*, par. 3.
[16] *Ibid*, par. 5.
[17] *Ibid*, par. 11.

CHAPTER 6

Treasure in Earthen Vessels

It has become apparent that none of the theories was adequate for the task. The reality is larger than any human concept of it. Man's attempts to confine God's redemptive act to human, formal constructs inevitably led to ambiguity and distortion. Each concept as metaphor had its own contribution to make to our understanding—so long as we did not confuse the metaphor with the reality. But it was apparently never easy to restrain the urge to push the literary figures too far.

Probably if we pooled the contributions of all of the various speech figures, we would come closer to the truth. In the writings of Ellen White such a combining seems to occur. Her writings contain statements suggesting almost every one of the older atonement theories. In some cases several of them appear together—even in the same paragraph—without apparent consciousness of the historic struggles those ideas represented. For example, consider the following quotations:

> On the cross of Calvary He paid the redemption price of the race. And thus He gained the right to rescue the captives from the grasp of the great deceiver. . . . Satan refused to let his captives go. He held them as his subjects because of their belief of his lie. He had thus become their jailor.[1]
>
> The world does not acknowledge that, at an infinite cost, Christ has purchased the human race. They do not acknowledge that by creation and by redemption He holds a just claim to every human being. But as the Redeemer of the fallen race, He has been given the deed of possession, which entitles Him to claim them as His property.[2]

We have here an almost classic expression of the transaction theory. To her credit, however, nowhere does she use those ancient gross figures of speech: net, trap, bait, et cetera.

A number of her expressions of the moral influence theory

would have certainly pleased Abelard: "This was to be God's means of winning men to Him."³

> Through the cross, man was drawn to God. . . . Through the cross the sinner was drawn from the stronghold of sin, from the confederacy of evil, and at every approach to the cross his heart relents and in penitence he cries, "It was my sins that crucified the Son of God." At the cross he leaves his sins, and through the grace of Christ his character is transformed.⁴
>
> As the sinner is drawn to the dying Christ, he sees the grievous character of sin, and repents and lays hold on the remedy, the Lamb of God, who taketh away the sin of the world.⁵
>
> If the cross does not find an influence in its favor, it creates an influence. . . . Christ on the cross was the medium whereby mercy and truth met together, and righteousness and peace kissed each other. This is the means that is to move the world.⁶

Something equivalent to the mystical or identification theory appears frequently.

> Those who have united their interests in love with Christ are accepted in the Beloved. They suffer with Christ, and His glorification is of great interest to them, because they are accepted in Him. God loves them as He loves His Son.⁷

Ellen White frequently uses the word *satisfaction* in her discussions of the atonement. Sometimes it is God who is satisfied (Anselm). "The Father accepts His Son. No language could convey the rejoicing of heaven or God's expression of satisfaction and delight in His only-begotten Son, as He saw the completion of the atonement."⁸

"He [the Father] is satisfied with the atonement made."⁹

Most often she portrays it as abstract justice that is satisfied (the forensic Reformers). "Justice is satisfied. Those who believe in Christ, those who realize that they are sinners, and that as sinners they must confess their sins, will receive pardon full and free." [10]

"Justice demanded that a certain price is paid. The Son of God was the only One who could pay this price." [11]

"With perfect satisfaction Justice bowed in reverence at the cross, saying, It is enough." [12]

> Justice demands that sin be not merely pardoned, but the death penalty must be executed. God, in the gift of His only begotten Son, met both these requirements. By dying in man's stead, Christ exhausted the penalty and provided a pardon.[13]

In a number of passages Ellen White attested the governmental principle. "The object of this atonement was that the divine law and government might be maintained. . . . There is forgiveness of sin, and yet the law of God stands immutable, eternal as His throne." [14]

"The cross must occupy the central place because it is the means of man's atonement and because of the influence it exerts on every part of the divine government." [15] (Notice just a touch of Abelard here also.)

We even find references suggesting an early theory of the atonement to which we drew attention only in passing in our brief survey of the history of the idea—Irenaeus' recapitulation theory. "The Son of God was the only one who could pay the price. He volunteered to come to this earth and pass over the ground where Adam fell." [16]

Sometimes she mixes the metaphors together.

> What right had Christ to take the captives out of the enemy's hands [transaction]? The right of having made a sacrifice that satisfies the principles of justice [forensic] by which the kingdom of

heaven is governed [governmental].[17]

All of which serves to make the essensial point both for Ellen White and for the Bible (where we find similar examples). So exalted a theme can be approached by, but must not be limited to, language. Metaphor is the appropriate medium, but we must never push it beyond its appropriate function. Like flowers, living figures of speech are killed when we press them into formal theories. Ellen White was quite clear that the cross is an exhaustless theme and will occupy our interest for a long time to come. "What a sacrifice is this! Who can fathom it! It will take the whole of eternity for man to understand the plan of redemption. It will open to him line upon line, here a little and there a little."[18]

This means that, at least for the present (the whole of eternity is an extremely long time), no one can claim finality for any particular concept—not the Bible writers, not the theologians, not the Reformers, not Ellen G. White—and certainly not any of us. That unfolding "line upon line" suggests that our efforts to understand are not misplaced, however. It is just that we must maintain at least a semblance of humility as we pursue this truth.

Nor does it signify that we cannot expect great assistance from inspired and even uninspired sources. It is only that we must not allow the sources to close the door on our quest. God gave inspiration to open doors, not to shut them. The inspired material provides a theme, and guidelines, general directions, and "checkpoints" against which we may plot our progress.

While there remains much to discover, some things are presently established. These function as guideposts to our understanding. Absolute truth may ever continue to elude us.

All that "present truth" demands is that our beliefs be consistent with one another. That is, in terms of our present interest, if our conceptions regarding why Christ died do not harmonize with established certainties, then we must either reject our theories or reformulate them until they do.

What are the certainties? They consist of at least the following: *God is one.* The oneness of God is not so much a quantitative expression as a qualitative one. It has to do with His character rather than number. Oneness means that God is always self-consistent, never contradictory. His specific actions may change as different needs and circumstances condition them, but there is never variability, "neither shadow of turning," in His essential character and purpose from one age to another. God's heart is always the same. For instance, the Bible does not depict two different Gods—one of Old Testament justice, the other of New Testament mercy. They are the same—one God.

Oneness extends to the Father and the Son. Jesus said, "He that hath seen me hath seen the Father." The Father and Son are qualitatively the same. What we may say about the character and purpose of One applies also to the Other. Essentially they are interchangeable as they interact with the creation they have brought into being and seek to restore. If One is loving, forgiving, noncondemning, compassionate, so must the other be. And if One shows firmness when love indicates, so must the other. In short, God is like Jesus, and that is just about the most important and wonderful news there can be.

Such oneness also applies to the creation as it expresses the character of its Creator. God who is one has created an orderly universe that is self-consistent and harmonious. True, sin has distorted it so that it no longer clearly reflects its divine origin in all respects—but it does so in its *essential* nature. The universe is a "lawful" place, and thus its creatures find safety and fulfillment—especially man if he is in harmony with the creation. Without is chaos, destruction, and death.

The orderliness of the universe is an expression of its Creator—who is self-consistent, one. God cannot break its real laws without violating Himself. This does not mean that God is bound by something higher than Himself—be it law, justice, or whatever. He is bound only by the nature of His own being. He is the Creator. Nor does it rule out the possibility of change or novelty, of doing things in different ways. God as Creator is in charge of His creation. Given legitimate options—that is, more than one orderly way of doing something—He can select, but He cannot choose disorder or chaos because, by definition, He is one. Thus in His universe causes *always* produce their effects. He may introduce new causes, but the new effects of the new causes will surely follow. It is just that God cannot act in a disorderly or chaotic way—and still be God. The reasons for our stressing this will become apparent shortly.

We must add one final point. When we say God is one, we also say that God is good. For this is essentially what we mean by good. God is self-consistent, fulfilling, creative, nondestructive, and harmonious—in a word, *orderly.* He also expresses those qualities toward His creation. They define love. He is *one* with His creation and is always loving and gracious toward it—by definition. And while He may exhibit His essential goodness in manifold ways, goodness itself is eternal and unchanging. God is eternally one, and God is eternally good. They amount to the same thing.

[1] Ellen G. White letter 20, 1903.
[2] ———, Letter 136, 1902.
[3] ———, Manuscript 165, 1899.
[4] ———, in *Signs of the Times*, June 5, 1893.
[5] ———, in *Review and Herald*, Sept. 2, 1890.
[6] ———, Manuscript 56, 1899.
[7] ———, in *Signs of the Times*, Aug. 16, 1899.
[8] *Ibid.*
[9] Ellen G. White, *Testimonies* (Mountain View, Calif.: Pacific Press Pub. Assn., 1948), vol. 6, p. 364.
[10] ———, Letter 52, 1906.
[11] ———, Letter 20, 1903.
[12] ———, in *General Conference Bulletin*, Fourth Quarter, 1899, vol. 3, p. 102.
[13] ———, Manuscript 50, 1900.
[14] ———, Manuscript 163, 1897.
[15] ———, *Testimonies*, vol. 6, p. 236.
[16] ———, Letter 20, 1903.
[17] ———, in *Signs of the Times*, Sept. 30, 1903.
[18] ———, Manuscript 21, 1895.

CHAPTER 7

Clouded Windows

Now, if what we have just said is true—and it *is* supported by the ultimate disclosure of the divine character in Jesus—we can begin to see certain deficiencies in some of the things that men have said about why Christ died. We may spend eternity learning about what our redemption is, but we can surely even now discover some of the things it is not. And that discovery might be most important.

What, for example, does the oneness of God have to say about the transactional theory of the atonement?

First off, it denies all intimations of deception on God's part. God could not be self-consistent and Himself do what He condemned in us. To be the God of order and integrity does not place Him above such qualities. As John Greenleaf Whittier wrote in his poem "The Eternal Goodness,"

> Not mine to look where cherubim
> And seraphs may not see,
> But nothing can be good in Him
> Which evil is in me.

As to the rest of the ransom narrative, it is strange that its proponents did not observe its inconsistency with God's way revealed earlier in Jesus. If Jesus is the clearest revelation of God, then God surely does not stoop to winning the world by bargaining with Satan. Recall Jesus' response to Satan in the wilderness temptation when the devil offered Him a transactional shortcut to rulership of the world (Luke 4:5-9). Satan has no such power against God.

As to the moral influence theory, Abelard's concept is not wrong so much as it is deficient. Abelard did not appreciate how deep runs the current of evil in all of us, nor did he perceive the cosmic scope of the great controversy between good and evil, involving a whole universe. His theory was correct as far as it went, but it was superficial and partial. There is more—a great deal more. The same could be said of the rectoral or governmental theory.

The satisfaction and forensic theories tended to obscure God's oneness in a number of ways, depending on the individual interpreter. They, for example, contrasted the Father and the Son. The One, the loving, compassionate, forgiving Son, offered His life to the Other, the angry Father, as a sacrificial appeasement designed to placate the Father's wrath. Probably no reputable theologian out of the past would acknowledge the concept stated in precisely those terms and would hasten to add that the Father Himself, in love, provided the sacrifice (but to appease Himself?). But nontheologians in whatever age have always found it easy to draw such a distinction between the Father and the Son.

And that is precisely the picture of the Father that Jesus came into the world to dispel! The Old Testament (and the New) do indeed have much to say about God's wrath. But the revelation in Jesus demonstrated that when applied to God the words *anger* and *wrath* have quite different connotations from what is intended when applied to man. If Jesus is a vision of God, God does not even experience the emotions to which we usually apply those terms, which among human beings often express hostility, wounded pride, and self-defensiveness.

Such a picture of God tends to reduce the whole to a pagan exercise. Pagan sacrifice assumes that the gods are against us and must be bought off or manipulated in our favor. The sacrifice is manipulative magic.

The history of the Old Testament sacrificial system illustrates what can happen to even good metaphors. Ritual sacrifices (pagan by the above definition) were common in and around

Palestine in the days of the children of Israel. But important differences existed between them and the Levitical code, however. We have reason to believe that the Israelites were at first involved in an almost mystical identification with the animals they offered for their sins. Thus their sacrifices stood proleptically for the eventual sacrifice of the Lamb of God and prepared them for the recognition of the role of Christ when He came. In the course of time, however, an essentially Christian concept of the atonement degenerated into something indistinguishable from its pagan counterparts—except for the superficial trappings.

Ellen White states that

> the people of Israel had not understood the lesson. Many of them regarded the sacrificial offerings much as the heathen looked upon their sacrifices—as gifts by which they themselves might propitiate the Deity. God desired to teach them that from His own love comes the gift which reconciles them to Himself.[1]

"Not only the things of nature, but the sacrificial service and the Scriptures themselves—all given to reveal God—were so perverted that they became the means of concealing Him."[2]

Apparently there is no guarantee that the meaning of a metaphor will not transmute into something quite different—even while using identical symbolic expressions.

The fact that a metaphor can be misused does not mean that there is anything intrinsically wrong with the metaphor itself. That the early Fathers of the church perceived ransom and redemption in terms of a sharp-bargaining Divine Merchant in no way empties the notion of its value content. The facts are, as sinners we are in bondage—and, in important ways, through no fault of our own. But it is no external condition that can be dealt with at some distant bargaining table. The trouble is in me! The "demons" are in me, in my character traits and behavior patterns, in my distorted will and perceptions. Jesus made His gracious disclosure to free me from such demons. (We shall say more about this later as we try to comprehend the deeper sin problem.)

To speak of satisfaction as appeasement of God or as meeting the requirements of abstract justice is to fail to be aware of the other ways in which what Christ did was satisfactory. "He shall see of the travail of his soul, and shall be satisfied," Isaiah wrote (chap. 53:11). Such satisfaction can mean "It was worth it!" or it can mean the travail was sufficient or adequate to the situation. It doesn't have to mean that God was appeased or mollified.

Note the direction of the following statements by Ellen White:

"He ascended to the heavenly courts, and from God Himself heard the assurance that His atonement for the sins of men *had been ample.*" (Italics supplied.)[3]

"With perfect satisfaction Justice bowed in reverence at the cross, saying, *It is enough.*"[4] (Italics supplied.)

"His sacrifice is *in every way satisfactory.*"[5] (Italics supplied.)

"The sacrifice in our behalf was *complete.*"[6] (Italics supplied.)

It is only fair to note that Ellen White's general thrust on this point, however, reasserts what Anselm, the Reformers, and others had said. Nor would it be correct to suggest that she perceived all the theological difficulties those positions projected. Also it is unrealistic to expect total consistency in one who was primarily in the tradition of the prophets rather than of the systematic theologians.

It is the forensic theory that runs most quickly into conflict with the proposed guidelines about God. The notion of satisfying justice, whether in God or as an abstraction, presupposes an understanding of what one means by it—and justice can connote several different things.

The legal presuppositions of the Reformers included an equity theory whose roots ran deep into almost every ancient judicial system. In its most primitive form it is *lex talionis*—the law of the talion (we derive the word *retaliation* from this term). Simply stated, it says, "An eye for an eye, and a tooth for a tooth." On these terms, punishment suited to the crime, not only equitably but unremittingly, serves justice. A strict application of the principle requires that punishment *always* be given. To withhold what the offender deserves is to commit an act of injustice. And it must be dispensed simply because the person who has broken the law deserves it—and for no other reason. *Lex talionis* opposes any utilitarian use of punishment solely for deterrent, for reformation, for rehabilitation, or for educational purposes. One does not punish to make things better, but because justice requires it. One may, of course, "punish" for these other reasons, as well, but such punishment falls outside the domain of justice. (Probably another word such as *education* would be more appropriate in that case.)

The concept we have described is retributive justice. It is the most fundamental, primitive understanding of justice known and usually prevails in somewhat unsettled communities.

A contrasting form of justice, as it relates to the question at hand, suits the punishment not so much to the crime as to the criminal. It has as its proper end the serving of the real needs of the one who has committed the criminal act and seeks his possible betterment. This concept of justice takes into account such things as the kind of person the criminal is. Is he hardened? Is this his first offense? Is he sorry? Was his act willful? Will he likely do it again? Has he learned his lesson? Such justice assumes that some persons are more or less deserving of punishment than others—in fact, that some may even merit it not at all. The remission of punishment for good reasons, on these terms, does not violate justice. It may even serve it. The key expression for this form of justice is "To each that which belongs to him," "To each his own." The label is distributive justice.

In our complex, sometimes violent, world, the two concepts of justice have found themselves in tension with each other. For example, in California the former practice of granting indeterminate sentences to convicted felons, supposedly based on an enlightened penal system designed to rehabilitate rather than merely punish or deter, has lately fallen into legal disrepute. The reason given is that far too many ex-felons were being paroled into society, only to repeat their violent behavior. Officials trying to operate the system became aware that the indeterminate sentence had turned every convict into a "con artist" intent on convincing prison officials and parole boards that he had been rehabilitated. And parole boards simply did not possess the divine vision required to peer into the individual's often twisted inner soul. As a consequence, California has turned toward predetermined sentences, and thus away from distributive justice to retribution—from punishment tailored to the criminal to punishment fitting the crime. Whether this will reduce the recidivism rate remains to be seen.

What concept of justice is appropriate to the question at hand? Obviously, the usual forensic formulation of the atonement presupposes retributive justice. On its terms the wages (penalty) for sin is death, and God cannot remit the penalty without violating the just principle upon which His kingdom rests. Since all have sinned, all too must die. But God wills, in love, to save man. Therefore He provides a substitute in the form of His Son, who, because of who He is, more than makes up for the whole human race. His Son dies in man's stead, freeing man from the penalty. All heaven rejoices—and security reigns throughout the kingdom of heaven because justice has been served as well as love and mercy.

And we run squarely into Bozo again! Does not such an explanation in principle actually jeopardize the security of God's government in the long run? How can so blatantly unjust an act actually serve justice? We face other questions, as well. If the justice that is met is God's, is it not strange that He must serve Himself by His own Gift? But if justice is outside God as an abstract principle, then there is something higher than God that He must also bow before—a "god" beyond God.

Also, we must come to grips with the issue of the penalty. By it we usually mean the ultimate, final death—the second death that Jesus died and from which He freed the sinner. But the human Jesus did not literally die the second death. He tasted of its agony—the aloneness of it. Our Saviour "died" it by subjective experience, but by definition there is no resurrection from the second death. In fact, He, as God, did not even die the first death! Deity is by nature immortal. Ellen White reminds us, "Deity did not die. Humanity died, but Christ now proclaims over the rent sepulcher of Joseph, 'I am the resurrection, and the life.' " [7]

If in His humanity He was truly human, then a man died on the cross—the first death. But is that what the theologians had in mind when they talked of a legally *adequate* substitute? Can a *man* literally die for all of humanity, or only for himself?—in this case not even for Himself, since He did not deserve to die. And, of course, there still remains the question of the confusion between criminal and civil law, to which we referred earlier.

In all this it becomes apparent that justice as "an eye for an eye, and a tooth for a tooth," simply is an inadequate explanation as to why Christ had to die. And we should have guessed it. Jesus Himself repudiated the principle.

> Ye have heard that it hath been said, An eye for an eye, and a tooth for a tooth: but I say unto you, That ye resist not evil.... Love your enemies, bless them that curse you, do good to them that hate you, and pray for them which despitefully use you, and persecute you that ye may be the children of your Father which is in heaven. (Matt. 5:38-44).

Did Jesus here advocate the renunciation of justice? No. Rather, He called men to divine justice, involving love, mercy, and forgiveness. It is the justice of the new kingdom. Justice and mercy unite in God.

The reason indeterminate sentences have seemed ineffectual, apparently even dangerous to society, has been that they called for human prison officials and parole boards to judge the hearts of the inmates applying for parole. It is on this basis that human justice must have in it so large an element of retribution. Acts are easier to judge than are people.

But God is under no such limitations. "The Lord looketh on the heart" (1 Sam. 16:7). Only He can accurately appraise a man. It is thus a part of God's justice to forgive and to accept a repentant sinner. In fact, it would be the height of injustice for Him not to do so. A man who longs for the arms of God *ought* to be in them. He belongs there.

But to understand this we must first grasp what it means to say that a man is a sinner who can justly be forgiven. Otherwise we shall be left with a contradiction of terms. The statement is not contradictory. God who is *one* cannot by definition contradict Himself. The harmony of this statement we will discover as we come to understand what we mean when we say man is a sinner. And this expression, too, has its own history.

[1] Ellen G. White, *The Desire of Ages* (Mountain View, Calif.: Pacific Press Pub. Assn., 1940), p. 113.
[2] ———, *Christ's Object Lessons* (Washington, D.C.: Review and Herald Pub. Assn., 1941), p. 18.
[3] ———, *The Desire of Ages*, p. 790.
[4] ———, in *General Conference Bulletin*, Fourth Quarter, 1899, vol. 3, p. 102.
[5] ———, in *Signs of the Times*, Aug. 16, 1899.
[6] ———, *The Ministry of Healing* (Mountain View, Calif.: Pacific Press Pub. Assn., 1942), p. 451.
[7] ———, in *The SDA Bible Commentary* (Washington, D.C.: Review and Herald Pub. Assn., 1956), vol. 5, p. 1113.

CHAPTER 8

The Darkness Behind the Shadows

Any response to the question "Why did Christ have to die?" which takes the form "To save us from our sins" presupposes an understanding of sin. That response is both Biblical and traditional. The angel announced to Joseph, "He shall save his people from their sins" (Matt. 1:21), and Paul wrote in that well-known passage in his letter to the Romans, "But God commendeth his love toward us, in that, while we were yet sinners, Christ died for us." (chap. 5:8). And, of course, the cross has been the central fact of man's salvation from sin in Christian preaching and writing ever since.

But to say this is not to declare something that is necessarily obvious. Sin is not a simple notion—certainly not in today's parlance. Bertrand Russell once wrote, "Although the *sense* of sin is easy to recognize and define, the *concept* of sin is obscure, especially if we attempt to interpret it in nontheological terms."[1]

The problem exists even more today. Ours is a world generally no longer on speaking terms with such old-fashioned "God language." Frederic Greeves observes:

> It is doubtful whether most Christians fully recognize that sin is a word that belongs to the religious vocabulary and has ceased to be a meaningful and active concept in the minds of those who do not read the Bible or attend church services.[2]

According to Gustav Aulen, "Sin is a concept which cannot be used except in a religious sense."[3]

Presbyterian, Sunday school teacher, dean of American psychiatrists, Karl Menninger recently wrote a book entitled *Whatever Became of Sin?* In it he says:

> In all of the laments and reproaches made by our seers and prophets, one misses any mention of "sin," a word which used to be a veritable watchword of prophets. It was a word

once in everyone's mind, but now rarely if ever heard. Does that mean that no sin is involved in all our troubles—sin with an "I" in the middle? Is no one any longer guilty of anything? Guilty perhaps of a sin that could be repented and repaired or atoned for? Is it only that someone may be stupid or sick or criminal—or asleep? Wrong things are being done, we know; tares are being sown in the wheat field at night. But is no one responsible, no one answerable for these acts? Anxiety and depression we all acknowledge, and even vague guilt feelings; but has no one committed any sins?

Where, indeed, did sin go? What became of it?[4]

It is surely nothing new that men want to get away from acknowledging their sins or even thinking about them. Is this not the religious history of mankind? Perhaps we are only more glib nowadays and equipped with more euphemisms. We can speak of error and transgression and infraction and mistakes without the naive exposure that goes with serious use of that old-fashioned pietistic word "sin.". . . When I was a boy, sin was still a serious matter and the word was not a jocular term. But I saw this change; I saw it go. I am afraid I even joined in hailing its going.[5]

Interestingly, while the Bible says a great deal about sin and provides an abundance of sometimes unsettling illustrations, it makes little attempt at formal definition. Jesus didn't define it. Astonishingly, He used the word barely a half dozen or so times. Mostly, Jesus illustrated sin by directing attention to the behavior and attitudes of people of His day who were sinners—and surprisingly influential and admired people they often were, too. He went beneath the surface of the act to intention and motivation behind it, but never once gave us a true, formal definition.

Paul provides a somewhat negative definition in Romans

14:23: "Whatsoever is not of faith is sin." John wrote in 1 John 3:4, "Sin is the transgression of the law," and thus seemed to say that *sinful* is synonymous with *unethical.* We could, of course, interpret the law in terms of reality itself rather than merely by specific rules and moral pronouncements. To transgress the law could mean to be out of harmony with the way things really are (see Chapter 1). In which case to sin could be infinitely complex, involving considerably more subtle and sweeping possibilities than such obvious matters as lying or having a secret affair with your best friend's wife. The way things are does not always float easily on the surface.

Such a definition would be consonant with the long-held notion that sin is always in some way against God. In the words of Frederic Greeves:

> Whatever else the Christian may mean when he speaks of sin, he most certainly refers to the relationship between man and God. . . . He may speak of disobedience or transgression, of rebellion and consequent alienation, of self-dependence or self-centeredness, he may describe the "root," or the "essence" of sin in many diverse ways; he cannot complete any statement about the nature of sin without reference to God.[6]

Augustine, the most influential early theologian after Paul, defined sin as follows: "What is the origin of our evil will but pride? For 'pride is the beginning of sin.' And what is pride but the craving for undue exaltations? . . . When the soul abandons Him to whom it ought to cleave."[7] And again, "flesh is good; but to leave the creator good and live according to this created good is not good."[8]

Thomas Aquinas wrote that "It is common to all sins to

be against God."[9] The basis for such sin Thomas viewed as the inordinate love of self.[10]

Luther used pride and self-love interchangeably, but saw their beginning in departure from God. "The wise man has said: 'The beginning of all sin is to depart from God and not trust Him.'"[11]

Calvin followed Paul in Romans 1 in saying that not ignorance but pride, especially intellectual pride, is sin.

> They worship not Him but figments of their own brains instead. This pravity Paul expressly remarks: Professing themselves wise, they became fools. He had before said they became vain in their imaginations. But lest any should exculpate them, he adds that they were deservedly blinded, because, not content with the bounds of sobriety, but arrogating themselves more than was right they wilfully darkened and even infatuated themselves with pride, vanity and perverseness. Whence it follows that their folly is inexcusable, which originates not only in a vain curiosity but in false confidence and in immoderate desire to exceed the limits of human knowledge.[12]

Some of the early Greek Church Fathers referred to sin in terms of sensuality and especially sexual license. And, of course, they were not unique in doing so. Christians have always found it easy to place sexual behavior at the top of the sin list. It is no accident that the terms *moral* and *sexual* are almost interchangeable expressions. Moral offenses usually do not involve "nice, clean crimes" like robbing banks. Possibly this fact has something to do with the power and universality of the allurement to sensual pleasure. (How many of us are tempted to rob banks?)

In Origen's concept of the Fall, the serpent physically

seduced Eve, infecting her with an inclination "to ignominy and wantonness." His belief led him to renounce all sexual activity as inherently evil and the ground of all sins. Clement of Alexandria and Gregory of Nyssa both associated the Fall with sexuality. Gregory even suggested that the fact that God created humans bisexual indicated a divine anticipation of, and preparation for, the Fall.

Augustine's negative attitude toward sexuality is well known. The behavior of his earlier years, his Christian mother's entreaties, and his nine-year fling with Manichaeism in which all things physical bore a negative value, probably conditioned him. But he and his followers tended to agree with Paul in Romans 1 that sensuality and lust were sinful, but at a secondary level rather than as the original fault. Augustine wrote in *The City of God*:

> If any man say that flesh is the cause of the viciousness of the soul, he is ignorant of man's nature, for the corruptible body does not burden the soul.—For this corruption that is so burdensome to the soul is *punishment* for the first sin and not the cause. The corruptible flesh made not the soul to sin, but the sinning soul made the flesh corruptible; from which corruption although there arise some incitements to sin, and some vicious desires, yet are not all sins of an evil life to be laid to the flesh, otherwise we shall make the devil, who has no flesh, sinless.[13] [Italics supplied.]

Thomas Aquinas defined original sin as concupiscence, but even he insisted that concupiscence came about by self-love. "In this repect, every sinful act proceeds from inordinate desire for some temporal good," he wrote. "Now the fact that anyone desires a temporal good inordinately is due to the fact that he loves himself inordinately."[14] Luther agreed. *Lust*, a word he employed as an all-inclusive word for sin in terms of its narrower, sensual definition, he saw as a consequence of man's prideful turning away from God. Sensual lust comes into being when one loves self rather than God.

What is of interest to us here is the quest for some condition or state that serves as the root of sinful behavior, including sensual activity—"the sin behind the sins," "the darkness behind the shadows." Most of the theories about why Christ had to die seem to be primarily concerned with that underlying condition.

All these great figures seemed to realize with Paul how deep runs the stream of evil in each of us, how bound to sin we are even when we would be free. They understood well the anguished frustration Paul expressed in Romans 7:14-24 (R.S.V.):

> I am carnal, sold under sin. I do not understand my own actions. For I do not do what I want, but I do the very thing I hate. . . . Nothing good dwells within me. . . . I can will what is right, but I cannot do it. For I do not do the good I want, but the evil I do not want is what I do. . . . I delight in the law of God, in my inmost self, but I see in my members another law at war with the law of my mind and making me captive to the law of sin which dwells in my members. Wretched man that I am! Who will deliver me from this body of death?

All of us almost always *know* better than we *do*. What is there about us that appears inevitably to foredoom our best efforts to reach our ideals? And what is it that from our earliest dawnings of conscious awareness seems to trip us up in spite of our best intentions and will to do better—even the best of us—individually and together?

Those with a bent for theological explanations have historically been quick to jump to a simplistic grasp of that really quite complicated statement of Paul in Romans 5:12, "Wherefore, as by one man sin entered into the world, and death by sin; and so death passed upon all men, for that all have sinned," and have offered it as an answer. We were born this way! "Behold, I was shapen in iniquity; and in sin did my mother conceive me," the psalmist had said (Ps. 51:5). And he was right. We know it as we look at ourselves and at one another—and at our children.

It would be a mistake, of course, to read into such theologians' thought forms and questions our contemporary ways of looking at things—or to criticize them on that basis. They proposed their answers long before anyone had elaborated the psychodynamics of human behavior, the mechanics of genetics and heredity, the process of acquiring characteristics, and the like in our terms. But the facts are that, without the assistance of Gregor Johann Mendel, Sigmund Freud, and Thomas Watson, our spiritual ancestors knew well that prior to the act there exists a predisposition to act.

They tended to distinguish between this predisposition (original sin) and the act (actual sin)—the former imposed upon us through no fault of our own, the latter the result of our own willful choice. However, the term *predisposition* is not quite accurate for all of them. For some, original sin was an objective state or legal status into which our first parents' sin thrust us.

We shall need to explore this tendency to think of sin in

objective, "thing" terms at some length, since it has deeply conditioned several of the theories as to why Christ had to die. It formed the conceptual base, for example, for the literalization of Biblical metaphor in the early transactional formula. When the Bible spoke of man's captivity to sin, as in the Pauline statement quoted earlier, "another . . . making me captive to the law of sin" (Rom. 7:23, R.S.V.), it was easy to translate this into a literal hostage situation. (Though not by all. Such literalism seems to be a habit of specific personalities. Apparently not everyone possesses the esthetic sensitivity required to correctly read figures of speech.)

Such literalism was not new. Long before the New Testament and the Church Fathers, at least some Hebrews probably conceived of their atonement ceremonial rituals in such literal terms. To them it did not seem incongruous to think of sins accumulating like debris in the tabernacle or later Temple. The high priest after going into the Holy of Holies on Yom Kippur, would transfer these sins onto the head of the Azazel goat, which carried them out into the wilderness. In like manner some of their later counterparts would see the Lamb of God as having our collective sins objectively off-loaded onto Him. His "bearing our sins" could have similar literal, objective implications.

Something of that objectification cropped up in the later theological notion of what Adam passed on to his progeny—*peccatum originale*, "original sin"—a term Frederic Greeves considers to be

> the most ill-chosen and unfortunate term in the whole Christian vocabulary. . . . Throughout Christian history there has been a

tendency to suggest that the responsibility for our sins can be laid on Adam, a tendency which is quite out of harmony with the New Testament. . . . The term *original sin* has increased the danger of treating sin as a *thing*.[15]

Note how this shows up in Aquinas' figure of the body, where

> all men born of Adam may be considered as one man inasmuch as they have one common nature, which they receive from their first parents; . . . Accordingly, the multitude of men born of Adam are *so many members of one body*. [Italics supplied.] Now the action of one member of the body, of the hand, for instance, is voluntary, not by the will of that hand, but by the will of the soul, the first mover of the members. Therefore a murder which the hand commits would not be imputed as a sin to the hand, considered by itself apart from the body, but is imputed to it as something belonging to man and moved by man's first moving principle. In this way, then, the disorder which is in this man born of Adam is voluntary, not by his will, but by the will of his first parent, who, by the movement of generation, moves all who originate from him, even as the soul's will moves all the members to their actions. Hence the sin which is transmitted by the first parent to his descendants is called *original*. . . . So original sin is not the sin of this person, except inasmuch as this person receives his nature from his first parent.[16]

Aquinas worried about Ezekiel's response to the proverbial saying in Israel, "The fathers have eaten sour grapes, and the children's teeth are set on edge" (chap. 18:2). Ezekiel had said, "The son shall not bear the iniquity of the father, neither shall the father bear the iniquity of the son" (verse 20). Therefore the great theologian argued that the son is said not to bear the iniquity of his father, because he is not punished for his father's sin, unless he share in his guilt. It is thus in the case before us, because guilt is transmitted by the way of origin from father to son, even as actual sin is transmitted through being imitated.[17]

A man is not blamed for that which he has from his origin, if the man born be considered in himself. But if we consider him as referred to a principle, then he may be reproached for it; and thus a man may from his birth be under a family disgrace because of a crime committed by one of his forebearers.[18]

Really now? That statement might have passed muster in the thirteenth century, but it mightily strains today's sense of fair play—and certainly overtaxes any rational understanding of the processes of heredity that any of us moderns know about.

The thirteenth century held to a number of biological notions that appear strange to us now, but Thomas Aquinas was correct in one sense in his reference to each individual man being a part of a body. It is a biological fact that an unbroken chain of cellular protoplasm reaches clear back to the primal man. Each of us is but the latest product of cellular division taking place ages ago in Adam.

But the question is Can sin or guilt be a function of cellular division—a *thing?* Such a notion has one advantage. One can deal with sin as a thing by "thing" acts—ceremonies, rituals, et cetera. (Still today, following ancient practice in the Roman Church, many Christians baptize infants as soon after birth as feasible. This may take place even before birth by means of a syringe if the probability exists that the infant will not survive delivery. Baptism in Roman Catholicism is concerned with inherited sin. Confession deals with actual sins. Thus having taken care of the "sin behind the sins" so easily, Roman Catholicism busies itself with acts and rules in an elaborate moral philosophy.)

And we can discover a similar base for those theories of why Christ had to die that develop the answer in external, mechanistic, ritualistic, even legalistic ways. Anytime we literalize such formulations out of their figurative significance, the corollary concept is sin as a thing. And if sin is an object, of course, it must be dealt with in *object* ways. Almost all of the classical atonement theories readily lend themselves to such crassly material interpretation. It is, to be sure, a risk we run when we use metaphor—we may strain the metaphor by literalizing it beyond its tolerable limits.

But to return to our subject, by what genetic witchcraft does an act of Adam become incorporated into the protoplasm we inherit from him? What exactly *do* we acquire from Adam? Is sin a *thing* quality, like blue eyes and blond hair or having pendulous ear lobes? Some interesting experiments performed in the laboratory with flatworms and mice suggest that learned behavior can in a measure transmit itself to other animals through injection or ingestion of RNA molecules derived from previously trained animals.[19] We are a long way yet from a complete understanding of all the processes of heredity. But is there an objective base for the transmission of sinful behavior patterns?

Undoubtedly, selection plays a role in the process. The destructive aggressiveness, self-defensiveness, and urge to compete and dominate that comprise so much a part of what we think of when we speak of sin might have survival value in a world that has turned Christian values on their heads. Throughout the struggle of human history the survivors have tended to possess just such characteristics. The nonsurvivors have, by contrast, been peace-loving and passive. Usually the unequal struggle has eliminated them—at least in the short run. Thus valid principles of natural selection might guarantee that most of us will have the instincts to kick our way lustily into the world.

Undoubtedly such factors, and probably a host of others that we haven't even begun to explore, work to make our children come out chips off the old block. They might explain, at least partially, what Adam passed on to his progeny, though such processes as natural selection might take many generations. (What got so quickly into Cain?) As our analysis proceeds it will be apparent that there are perhaps even more rational possibilities.

But the transmission of guilt? A *sense* of guilt, perhaps. We all know how easy it is to unload our guilty feelings upon others—including our own children. But how can Adam's sinful act render me *actually* guilty? (Recall that Ezekiel text.) I, frankly, had nothing to do with Adam's sin, nor did you, nor did anybody else. He did it on his own, and that's why he was guilty. Even the devil didn't *make* him do it.

At least three kinds of guilt concern us here. They are (1) real guilt, (2) false guilt, and (3) neurotic guilt.[20] Real guilt has to do with those acts or attitudes about which we *ought* to feel guilty. It is an emotional experience (difficult to describe but well known to us all) involving feelings of self-condemnation for having done things that we clearly believe to be wrong. How we come to label those things wrong, of course, may vary. While it may not be possible to *define* sin without reference to God, it certainly is possible for even a practicing atheist to *experience* guilt.

The intensity felt may depend upon the sensitivity of the person. Some people suffer real guilt over matters that others might consider quite trivial. Guilt so ravaged Martin Luther during the monastic phase of his life that he began to weary the vicar of his Augustinian monastery, Staupitz, with his compulsive confessions. Staupitz exclaimed, "Man, God is not angry with you. You are angry with God. Don't you know that God commands you to hope?" As Roland Bainton put it,

> This assiduous confessing certainly succeeded in clearing up any major transgressions. The leftovers with which Luther kept trotting in appeared to Staupitz to be only the scruples of a sick soul. "Look here," said he, "if you expect Christ to forgive you, come in with something to forgive—parricide, blasphemy, adultery—instead of all these peccadilloes."[21]

Probably Staupitz was correct, but it was a combination—real, false, and neurotic guilt—that hounded the Reformer day and night. It was also the anguish of an oversensitive conscience.

In the main, real guilt is a good thing when properly handled. It is analogous to pain. Pain is an important protective mechanism without which it might be impossible for us to survive. Diseases like syringomyelia and Hansen's disease (leprosy) so disrupt the sensation pathways that the patient feels no pain—with dire consequences. The finger and limb stumps of the late stages of Hansen's disease result largely because any trauma to these parts does not cause discomfort. Lepers come to think of their insensitive members as objects and use (or abuse) them accordingly.

As pain can deter us from misusing parts of our bodies, just so guilt can provide protection by warning us when we have violated the behavioral code we have come to accept as the way we ought to live.

We can push the analogy even further. Pain is good *up to a point!* When it serves its *proper* end it indicates that something is wrong and needs attention. But pain can also come to so dominate a disease that it becomes virtually a disease itself. Medical science has directed considerable research to finding ways of eliminating pain once it has accomplished its purpose. Just so the proper purpose of guilt feelings is to eradicate whatever causes them. Continuing to bear guilt when it should have been cleared away can result in the destructive behavior we often see in neurotic guilt.

False guilt is the *dis*-ease of self-depreciation we experience when we have no clear object of guilt. It is true, of course, that this is relative. Some unhappy individuals, because of their background and moral education, feel real guilt about things that others of us would call false. What is false in this case is not the guilt but the moral object or teaching. We can suffer real guilt in the presence of false objects of guilt. In false guilt, the feelings remain in spite of learning and logic. Persons enduring it may realize they shouldn't feel guilty, or even be unable to recall the guilt object(s)—as in free-floating guilt.

False guilt frequently has its roots in early infancy, when the subject picks up and internalizes his relative sense of value or disvalue from what he sees reflected in the faces of the persons in his life. It can also result from the conscious or unconscious guilt-loading of others struggling to cope with their own neurotic guilts. How often has a father transferred his own deep unresolved real and false guilts, compensated for, perhaps, by moralistic, self-righteous rigidity, into his son through his impossible demands! Such sons, loaded with guilt over not being able to measure up, have pleaded, "What does he want from me? I can never please him!" And, of course, that vicious cycle can go on for generation after generation.

How much of the guilt experienced in the following story by Karl Menninger was false?

> On a sunny day in September, 1972, a stern-faced, plainly dressed man could be seen standing still on a street corner in the busy Chicago Loop. As pedestrians hurried by on their way to lunch or business, he would solemnly lift his right arm, and pointing to the person nearest him, intone loudly the single word "GUILTY!"
>
> Then, without any change of expression, he would resume his stiff stance for a few moments before repeating the gesture. Then, again, the inexorable raising of his arm, the pointing, and the solemn pronouncing of the one word "GUILTY!"
>
> The effect of this strange *j'accuse* pantomime on the passing strangers was extraordinary, almost eerie. They would stare at him, hesitate, look away, look at each other, and then at him again; then hurriedly continue on their ways.
>
> One man, turning to another who was my informant, exclaimed: "But how did *he* know?"[22]

Was not much of that theological effort to tie us into Adam's guilt really a misplaced attempt to load us with, or at least rationalize, *false* guilt?

One thing real and false guilt have in common is that if

we do not handle them properly they become *neurotic guilt*. By neurotic guilt we refer to guilt that comes to wear a false face. One of the features of our humanness is our ability to cope with unpleasant and painful, threatening experiences by employing a variety of defensive mechanisms. These include repression, transference, denial, and avoidance (escape). We do not have to go on just enduring the pain, as an open, festering wound, day afer day. Such an ability often has survival value to the individual involved. How could anyone possibly live constantly exposed to the really terrible things some of us have to face without some kind of escape or release?

Unfortunately, not all of our mechanisms for coping are desirable. Indeed, some can be most destructive to ourselves and to others as we shall now see.

---

[1] Bertrand Russell, *Human Society in Ethics and Politics* (London: George Allen & Unwim, 1954), p. 89.
[2] Frederic Greeves, *The Meaning of Sin* (London: The Epworth Press, 1956), p. 3.
[3] *Ibid.*, p. 5.
[4] New York: Hawthorn Books, Inc., 1973, p. 13.
[5] *Ibid.*, p. 24.
[6] Greeves, *op. cit.*, p. 16.
[7] *The City of God*, Book XII, chap. 13.
[8] *Ibid.*, Book XIV, chap. 3, par. 5.
[9] *Summa* II (First Part), Q. 72, A. 4, rep. 1.
[10] *Ibid.*, I, No. 3, Q. 77, A. 4.
[11] *Treatise on Christian Liberty*, quoted in Reinhold Niebuhr, *The Nature and Destiny of Man* (New York: Charles Scribner's Sons, 1955), p. 183.
[12] *Institutes*, Book I, chap. 4, par. 1.
[13] *The City of God*, Book XIV, chap. 3.
[14] Aquinas, *op. cit.*, II (First Part), Q. 77, A. 4.
[15] Greeves, *op. cit.*, p. 31.
[16] Aquinas, *op. cit.*, II (First Part), Q. 81, A. 1.
[17] *Ibid.*, Q. 81, A. 1, rep. 1.
[18] *Ibid.*, rep. 5.
[19] In the late 1960s Hungarian-born neurochemist Georges Ungar jolted rats and mice with an electric shock whenever they wandered into a darkened box, eventually making the

normally nocturnal creatures afraid of the dark. The conditioned animals he then sacrificed and made their brains into a brew that he had injected into the peritoneal cavities of nonconditioned animals that subsequently, more often than not, also began to shun the dark. "Ungar and other researchers strongly suspect that the chemical mechanism for such learning is governed by RNA molecules in the brain cells. . . . Ungar is convinced that chemical processes similar to those in the brains of his rats also occur in the brains of higher animals, including man."—*Time*, Jan. 11, 1971, p. 34. We should add that not all scientists have completely accepted his work, because of the difficulty they experienced in duplicating his results.

[20] I am indebted to David Belgum for the three categories. See David Belgum, *Guilt: Where Religion and Psychology Meet* (Englewood Cliffs, N.J.: Prentice-Hall, Inc., 1963).

[21] *Here I Stand* (New York: Abingdon-Cokesbury Press, 1950), p. 54.

[22] Menninger, *op. cit.*, pp. 1, 2.

CHAPTER 9

Fig Leaves for the Naked

Not all of the theologians who addressed the question of why we all inevitably become sinners were as literalistic as Thomas Aquinas—or for that matter the Augustinians before him. They had insisted on interpreting original sin as an inherited taint. But Christian thought has always allowed room for the representative rather than historical character of Adam's sin. Very early some (Irenaeus, Ambrose) posited a mystical identity between Adam and all men. Adam sinned as representative man. (In much the same way the second Adam represents all those who are saved, a thought Paul expressed in Romans 5.)

Other ideas also struggled for expression. We see this even in some of Calvin's accounts of original sin. The Genevan Reformer clearly maintained a belief in inherited sin, but in one interesting passage he wrote, "For the children were so vitiated in their parent that they became *contagious* to their descendants."[1] (Italics supplied.) Calvin's thought here was a long way from Thomas Aquinas' "body" concept when he wrote this. Sinners by contagion and sinners by inheritance are notions that are poles apart.

Some theologians spoke of a bias toward sin. (Ellen White refers to "inherent propensities.")[2] And, of course, to receive a bias or propensity toward evil is not the same thing as inheriting real guilt.

Again the confusion seems to have resulted from thinking of sin in "thing" terms. But what if sin is not an object? What if what we are looking for in that darkness behind the shadows, the sin behind the sins, is a broken relationship, even an estrangement manifesting itself in objective ways, as observable actions, or "sins"? Wouldn't that refocus the picture?

To comprehend the nature of sin and its solution would require that we clearly understand man's relationship with

God—both before and after the Fall. Let us see what sin might mean on these terms.

The Bible's account of the sin of Adam[3] is marvelously instructive. The rebellion of Lucifer and his angels in heaven preceded Adam and Eve's sin. Unfortunately the Bible gives us little insight into Lucifer's moral catastrophe. We catch glimpses of a perfect creature in the figure of the king of Tyrus in Ezekiel 28, whose "heart was lifted up" because of his beauty and who said, "I will ascend into heaven, I will exalt my throne above the stars of God: I will sit also upon the mount of the congregation, in the sides of the north: I will ascend above the heights of the clouds; I will be like the most High" (Isa. 14:13, 14). Elsewhere we find allusion to "war in heaven," with the devil and his angels being cast out onto the earth (Rev. 12:7-9). Jesus spoke of seeing "Satan as lightning fall from heaven" (Luke 10:18), and the Bible gives ample space to his role of tempter of man and enemy of God. Such sketchy accounts give us some understanding of the nature of the heavenly rebellion, but little of its details.

Satan's fall has its main significance to us in that it suggests another fact for which the believers in original sin were searching, the fact that sin presupposes itself. There is sin before sin, although the Bible avoids suggesting, as did the Zoroastrians, that it extends infinitely back into the past. For the Bible it had to start sometime. What was the precondition of Satan's sin? Perhaps we shall never know. The Bible is silent.

As far as man is concerned, sin begins with Adam (at least in the New Testament reference that somewhat minimizes Eve's sin by deception—1 Timothy 2:14. The context suggests that this may be a bit of Pauline chauvinism, however. To Paul, Eve wasn't apparently even up to straight-out, open-faced sinning.

But the prototype of all masculine humanity, Adam was).

The Genesis account of the Fall is without question one of the richest pieces of literature in its depth of perception of the human situation. It begins with a created innocence. Everywhere existed harmony, peace, and tranquillity. And our primal parents were in charge of it all—except for two things. They were not absolutely in charge of time. One day in seven God set apart, hallowed, and sanctified to remind them that they were creatures of time. It was a day for celebrating God's creation. The other thing beyond their control was the "tree which is in the midst of the garden," known as the tree of knowledge of good and evil. It reminded them that creatureliness has limits in space, as well as in time. Both were reminders of man's creaturely finitude, while he exercised dominion over the world. Through such responsible, creaturely dependence Adam and Eve found the meaning of their existence. They were made for it. (You will recall that earlier we spoke of the transgression of the law in terms of being out of harmony with the way things are.)

In the Biblical story it is unclear why they became dissatisfied with things as they were. If theirs was truly a free act, one can speak only of the occasion, not the cause, of their choice. The Bible paints a picture of their being presented with two options—the one to transcend their creatureliness, to be "as gods," by eating the forbidden fruit; the other to continue in dependent obedience to their Creator.

The tree represented the possibility of death, whatever that might signify to someone inexperienced with death. (Was Eve's sin the original denial or rejection of death, a coping phenomenon wearing myriads of faces throughout human history? See the author's book *Is Death for Real?* [Mountain

View, California: Pacific Press Publishing Assn., 1981] for an expanded examination of this idea.) Since death in that setting might have little impact as a deterrent, what the options finally came to were Whom do you trust, the talking serpent or God? *The* original sin was thus an act of distrust of God. (We could also speculate something like this about the fall of Lucifer. Why should anyone aspire to be what he is not unless he rejects what he is? And to spurn what one is, is in effect to repudiate the One who made us the way we are. To reject one's creatureliness is in essence to distrust and to reject the Creator.)

Ellen White captures this thought in her statement in *Education,* page 25:

> There was nothing poisonous in the fruit itself, and the sin was not merely in yielding to appetite. It was distrust of God's goodness, disbelief of His word, and rejection of His authority, that made our first parents transgressors, and that brought into the world a knowledge of evil. It was this that opened the door to every species of falsehood and error.

Distrust lay not only at the heart of *the* original sin, it is the basis for much of what has occurred ever since. God made the creature for trustful, responsible dependence upon his Creator. At the tree he broke this bond.

The Genesis story is again instructive: As soon as Adam and Eve had eaten of the fruit "the eyes of them both were opened, and they knew that they were naked" (chap. 3:7). Here we find the first described experience of real guilt. "Naked" obviously refers to more than the mere lack of clothing. That fact hadn't changed. They hadn't worn clothes before. What was different was a new sense of vulnerability. Now they came to experience their nakedness in a new way—with shame.

A number of largely psychological terms could be used to describe the base for the defensive behavior expressed in what followed. In simplest terms they were alienated from God and from each other. Estranged and alone, they did not like themselves and turned on each other as they tried to shift the blame for their fallen estate. They were vulnerable and guilty—naked. Such expressions all point to that deep, inner disquiet that always goes with being out of harmony with the way things really are.

The Bible's portrayal of their response to their discovery is a page out of life as we even now experience it. Coping and behavior mechanisms were recognized long before depth psychology put labels on them. Almost instinctively our first parents tried to appear to be what they were not. The Bible says, "They sewed fig leaves together, and made themselves aprons" to cover their nakedness so that it would not show.

Ellen White writes:

> Naked and ashamed, they tried to supply the place of the heavenly garments by sewing together fig leaves for a covering.
> This is what the transgressors of God's law have done ever since the day of Adam and Eve's disobedience. They have sewed together fig leaves to cover the nakedness caused by transgression. They have worn the garments of their own devising, by works of their own they have tried to cover their sins, and make themselves acceptable with God.[4]

And, we might add, acceptable to themselves and to one another.

Fig leaves come in a variety of shapes and sizes. They include the almost infinite number of ruses men use to try to deal with their contemptuous inner view of themselves: the compensatory denials of weakness or its projection onto others; the status pride marks, material as well as moral, worn in the competitive struggle with the Joneses; all attempts to appear to be better than we see ourselves to be before the neighbors and before God—even before ourselves. Weakness advertises itself as strength, inferiority expresses itself as superiority, self-contempt tries to establish superior worth, guilt displays itself as moral self-righteousness, pride *(hubris)* appears in its countless forms (including false humility).

And the worst of it is that the ruses can give illusions of success. Denial can distort reality or repress it beneath the surface where one no longer has to look it in the face. Presumably, most people who parade their pride marks (whether of the material or of the self-righteous, moral variety) are unaware of the inner weakness that is their aegis—at least most of the time. We can lie to ourselves or to one another so often that we come to believe the deception, and in the process our defensive behavior produces neurotic guilt in which the causal link between our actions and the underlying failure is obscured. The symptoms come to appear not to belong to the disease. How many of the irrational, destructive things people do may be explained by deep, unresolved feelings of guilt and self-contempt? Though repressed beyond consciousness, they may break out in seemingly unrelated ways—even in somatic forms as bodily disease. And, of course, if we include all the other aspects of alienation from God—the total existential nakedness that characterizes man as sinner—we come to see something of what the Church Fathers were seeking in their notion of *peccatum originale*—the sin behind the sins—and that's what Romans 1:19ff. is about.

What the Genesis account reveals to us, then, is *an* original sin, distrust of God, resulting in a *state* of alienation from God. Out of distrust of God man became a sinner, and it is this underlying state that is the sin behind the sins.

It is not a condition that man shares only representatively with Adam. Every moment of his history he repeats it again and again in one way or another.

What is our relation to Adam, then? What of those inherited tendencies, propensities, and biases to sin? There remains some mystery as to the mechanisms by which one generation passes its acquired characteristics along to the next, but one thing seems clear. Inheritance is not limited to physiologic, genetic inheritance. Infants pick up through imprinting and cultural exposure many of their basic patterns early in life. And thus another aspect of that Genesis story takes on significance. When God discovered Adam and Eve hiding in the Garden and began to question them, each tried to unload his guilt onto the other—and onto the serpent. ("The devil made me do it.") And humanity has obvious, as well as subtle, even unconscious, ways of doing this. While *unloading* may not be the appropriate word, since the attempt to burden another with our guilt rarely lightens our own, it still may be useful in understanding the ease with which mankind passes the "nakedness" along.

But what is passed along is the anxiety of false guilt, not real guilt. Aquinas was wrong and Ezekiel right. But the consequences may be the same. Fancied nakedness can lead people to run for the fig leaves as surely as can real nakedness, and as surely may become the underlying basis for destructive neurotic behavior if unresolved. (False guilt can also become real guilt at the point where we choose it in the conscious presence of a divinely provided alternative.)

Original sin, then, on the above terms, is a broken

relationship, a state of alienation and estrangement and not a "thing." The attempts to cope with this state we may express as objective acts called sins, and these in turn may deepen the separation, creating a vicious cycle into which men may become locked and into which they may imprison others, including their children.

[1] *Institutes,* Book II, chap. 1, Par. 7.
[2] In *The SDA Bible Commentary,* vol. 5, p. 1128.
[3] This bit of negative chauvinism provides poetic balance to the general favor the Bible writers grant to males—the Bible books being all written by men, of course. Interestingly, some of our spiritual forefathers (for example, Aquinas) taught that the "principle of generation" comes only through the father's semen, therefore original sin could come only from Adam, not from Eve.
[4] *Christ's Object Lessons,* p. 311.

CHAPTER 10
A Truth Disclosed

It has always been easier to identify sins as surface objects than it has the more elusive and subtle sin behind them. It is also easier to attack them—even if generally it doesn't appear to change things much. In spite of all our best efforts to resist and control, our children continue to do their own things, crime rates soar, and nations plot against one another. Nakedness of heart can never really be plastered over with fig leaves—our own fig leaves or anyone else's—though we continue to try.

By contrast it is to the underlying *state* of brokenness that God primarily directs His saving grace, for if that alienation can be overcome and the separate united, the destructive coping behavior, the "sins," should become superfluous. Who will feel a compulsive urge to cover a guilt that no longer exists? Or who will need to prove his worth (materially or morally) to himself or to the neighbors (or to God) if the fact is not in question? Only what is in doubt has to be proved. Who will wish to escape from a fulfilled life? And who will cry out in loneliness and despair when wrapped in the gracious arms of His heavenly Father? Where there is no nakedness, neither will there be the need for fig-leaf aprons.

How one defines God's saving grace will also depend on how one considers the underlying state of sin to which it is directed. If we conceive of the state, on the one hand, in legal, objective "thing" terms, grace will also assume external, mechanical, objective legal characteristics. But if, on the other hand, we view sin in relational terms, grace will wear a personal, interactional face.

It is not that sin does not have its "objective" dimension. True, the past, in which those acts that manifest our estrangement from God occurred, does not exist objectively.

All we ever actually experience is the present moment, but we recall the past in present memory. Our minds store the act away as objective memory, shaping present relationships. An act committed against me is done and gone—but I remember it still, and its pain. I also continue to experience its lingering consequences. And so I do not trust you, and must protect myself. And such uneasiness will tinge the present moments of all in any way touched by the act, however remotely, vicariously, or otherwise. The past recalled can thus be the basis for present alienation, enmity, and distrust.

But how does one get a handle on a past that, in fact, does not exist? What's done is done. How many times have each of us cried out in anguish, "Oh, if I only had it to do over again!" But we cannot travel the road over again. As the poem says,

> Boys flying kites haul in their
>   white-winged birds;
> You can't do that way when you're
>   flying words.

We can deal only with the present. That's all any of us ever really have. And here we face at least two options. One is the way of punishment. "Give the wrongdoer his just desserts!" But why? So *we'll* feel better? Our best selves will always feel uneasy with the vindictiveness that option suggests. Will punishment undo the crime? It won't. What's done is done and cannot be undone. And afflicting an equivalent pain on the wrongdoer cannot undo that which he has caused—even though it might partially satisfy vengeful feelings in his victims. It might even provide some masochistic, emotional satisfaction to the wrongdoer if he's guilt-laden, and possibly deter him from further wrongful acts—hopefully. But will it overcome the estrangement between him and those he has wronged? Will he be trusted more after his punishment and be restored, to open houses and hearts again? No, not likely.

The other way is forgiveness. And in terms of a relational concept of sin, that's what God's grace is all about. He takes the sinner home again and restores him fully into the household, unequivocally, unconditionally. And only God can do it. It is a creative act, and He is the Creator.

But in doing so God does not rewrite history. What is done is done even for God. It may even be important in a universe honoring freedom to keep that history instructively available so that it will not be repeated. What God creates is a new relation with us sinners. There is sonship restored— and the past acquires a new meaning. The disturbing now refers to what we *were* and no longer to what we *are*. God's grace is His acceptance of the sinner as fully and completely as if he had never been away.[1] He can do that because He is God.

And that ought to end the matter. But, of course, it does not. The son must also wish to come home—and, in fact, actually move in that direction if he is to experience his restored sonship. The sinner must have a desire for restoration and accept the reinstatement given—deep in his inmost soul, whence the roots of his sinful acts spring, even those unconscious roots.

To *be* a son he must also come to *see* himself as a son. And the rest of the family and the neighbors must also acknowledge his sonship if that restoration is to include general openness and trust. A certain vulnerability goes with trust. One can have no doubts about someone to whom one chooses to become truly vulnerable.

But there's the rub! God's grace has no limit or deficiency. He offers it freely and unconditionally because He is God and it is one of His attributes to do so. Nothing has to be done to assist Him in offering His acceptance—nothing! It is total and a completely free, divine, creative act. (Free here is not synonymous with cheap, but in the sense of priceless. It is the delivery system—by which the sinner is made aware of His acceptance and is enabled to internalize it in his inner heart of hearts—that was so very, very expensive. And it involves nothing less than the laying bare of the infinite heart of God.)

The problem, then, lies not with God's grace, but with the sinner's lack of faith. If he could fully grasp what God's gracious acceptance of him really means, a transformation of his self-view and his relationships with his neighbors would instantly result. The symptoms would immediately disappear, because there is healing. What a joyous celebration.

But *can* he believe it? That is the question. And can his neighbors, not just at a surface level of assent, but down deep in total acceptance? Is it really so easy to lay one's guilts—including one's false and neurotic guilts—completely into God's hands and then rise from one's knees to have done with them, buoyant, released to creative joy?

Of course it isn't. Therapists know it, you know it, and God knows it. And we all continue to cling to self-condemnation (and its symptoms) when we should be rejoicing in the household of God!

God knows it and therefore has made provision for the

weakness of our faith. Among these provisions was information. Ignorant, we needed to know about Him. (Remember that the primary sin is always distrust.) We must come to realize that God is always on our side and that He is always trustworthy. He continually has our best good and eternal happiness in mind. It may take the whole of human history to demonstrate this fully—or at least until the consequences of the alternative to God's way have become adequately apparent. To teach this is the primary task of theology and an essential part of the gospel message.

We also needed to know something about ourselves, how God intended us to live. God's law describes His creation. Because we have become untrue to our essential selves, we especially must relearn this so that we may have insight into the destructive things we are doing to ourselves and to one another as we cope with the anxiety of our existential nakedness. We also, need to be informed as to the full consequences of following that destructive path.

And, finally, He had to present that information with such an impact that it would break the profound attitudinal bondage which is the slavery of sin so that we could choose a better way.

It is not enough merely to know intellectually that we are behaving as strangers, aliens, and slaves—when in fact we are the children of the King—to know that we could be free to enjoy the rich bounties of that heritage if we would but receive it in faith. Our slavery runs too deep for that. We do not have the power to accept freedom from our chains, even if we recognize their existence.

The problem is more than just propositional ignorance. Additional information could easily overcome that. Even if we knew of our heritage as a fact, it would not suffice to free us. Ours is the captivity experienced only by those who have come to perceive themselves in their own eyes as slaves. It is not merely informational servitude, it is *attitudinal* bondage.

In his important book, *Ethics and Language*,[2] Charles L. Stevenson makes a point of some relevance here. He distinguishes two kinds of disagreements: those of belief and those of attitude (not that they are mutually exclusive. One may affect the other. Belief may well shape attitude, and vice versa). The methods for dealing with the two kinds of disagreement differ. On the one hand, we overcome disagreements of belief by applying logic and additional data. On the other hand, when the disagreement involves attitudes, logic and cold facts are usually insufficient. (The person who says, "Don't confuse me with the facts; my mind is made up," exhibits attitudinal disagreement. So does the man who is convinced against his will.) Overcoming disagreements (estrangements?) of attitude requires the "loading" of logic and information in ways that stir the drives in the soul that lie deeper than mere surface intellect.

Ellen White referred to this fact when she wrote:

> The perception and appreciation of truth . . . depends less upon the mind than upon the heart. Truth must be received into the soul; it claims the homage of the will. If truth could be submitted to the reason alone, pride would be no hindrance in the way of its reception. But it is to be received through the work of grace in the heart; and its reception depends upon the renunciation of every sin that the Spirit of God reveals. Man's advantages for obtaining a knowledge of the truth, however great these may be, will prove of no benefit to him unless the

heart is open to receive the truth.³

It would not be enough for God to give us the cold facts about our true condition and about His gracious forgiveness and acceptance. Ours is not merely the alienation of ignorance. We are aliens in attitude, strangers in our hearts. And so He wrapped the facts in a warm and sensitive Life and bared them in all of the intensity and force that their truth could muster. He loaded the facts with heart-level reality—and then and only then did we become free to respond in faith.

The cross was that loading. But it was no dramatic overplay merely for the purpose of creating a moving effect. Abelard was wrong. God wasn't merely being winsome—even though He was that, too. He was telling the truth in the only way such truth could really reach the *hearts* of men and angels. And this truth was sufficiently loaded by its being accurately disclosed. The cross was the ultimate, forceful expression of the way things really are—it *is* the way things are!⁴

To explore that statement, let us look for a moment at some of the truths the cross revealed. It tells us that God is *one* in the sense discussed earlier. He is *one* in Jesus. God does not view the cross as the agony of someone else. The Father suffered with and in His Son! Theirs was a unity in suffering. "God was *in* Christ, reconciling the world unto himself" (2 Cor. 5:19).

And this suffering disclosed a truth about God. The book *Education* contains a statement that we have paid insufficient attention to:

> Few give thought to the suffering that sin has caused our

Creator. All heaven suffered in Christ's agony; but that suffering did not begin or end with His manifestation in humanity. The cross is a revelation to our dull senses of the pain that, from its very inception, sin has brought to the heart of God.[5]

As soon as there was sin, God was on the cross! And with every new sin we crucify Him afresh (Heb. 6:6). It is only that at Calvary's point in time and place the curtains pulled back so that our dim souls could behold what was always so since there was separation between God and His creation. God's heart was laid bare at the cross. The cross did not *make* anything so, but revealed what *was* so. The Lamb was slain "from the foundation of the world" (Rev. 13:8).

And what was so also includes a truth about ourselves—the depth of our sin. We crucified Him. And that is not just a rhetorical cliché. We, *you and I*, did it. Only an accident of time and space kept us from actually participating in the torture and murder of Calvary. You and I escaped by being born in the wrong century and perhaps the wrong country, but there are in us the same qualities that led those who crucified Him to behave as they did so long ago in Judea.

Many of us might have stood on the sidelines, as did they, and gawked as the soldiers dragged Him by. Many of the onlookers shouted, "Crucify him," but only a few of them actually touched Him. Most of them merely watched, but they all—and we together with them—crucified Him. And that's one answer to the question "Why did Jesus have to die?"

The cross disclosed still another truth about God. Not only is God *one* in the above sense, His oneness expresses itself in an *orderly* universe—a universe where causes always produce their effects (Professor Heisenberg notwithstanding). There is freedom and thus there are also *initiating* causes. Uncertainty may exist at the subatomic level but there is no freedom to destroy the causal sequence of things at least as they pertain to our lives. New causes can produce new effects and may thus even counter and modify previous causes and effects, but in a universe of law and order we cannot escape the inexorable principle that whatsoever we sow we shall also reap. (Although we may modify the reaping by another sowing. The cross could and did introduce new causes into the causal sequence.)

And sin is no exception. The cross is no clever device for getting around the orderliness of the universe. Instead it is the most profound expression of the truth that God is one, thus a God of order, that the world has yet seen. It revealed that *there is no getting around the law,* that the principle of cause and effect is profoundly and eternally at work in the universe.

God is on the cross when there is sin in the world, for when one loves deeply, one is also caused to suffer deeply by loss and rejection. The suffering is commensurate with the loving. God who loves more profoundly than anyone in all His universe also suffers the most intensely. Calvary in the first century was God's chosen way of imprinting that eternal fact upon our dull senses. What caused the death of Christ then? We caused it—all of us who "like sheep have gone astray; . . . every one to his own way" (Isa. 53:6).

And, of course, in this sense God has not finished with the cross even yet. Calvary was also a window on our present and future. Contemplate His sufferings at the final loss of those who would not return to Him after all that He could say was said and done forever.

The cross is thus a disclosure of the heart of God—that He is love preeminent. It also unveils another fact of His love—His grace. When Jesus pleaded for the forgiveness of those who were torturing Him, that too manifested the oneness of God. It was not the pleading of a gracious Saviour before an angry, righteous, and just God. (Remember there is no qualitative difference between them.) Jesus' words were God's words. *God* Himself was saying in that cry, "I forgive you—please accept My forgiveness so that you may be free from your compulsion to behave in this way." But they wouldn't listen to Him—and that was the real tragedy of that hour.

Calvary also reveals that such acceptance is absolutely free. Nobody has to (or can) pay for it or work for it. The cross rejects salvation by works *in principle*. It was a demonstration, not a payment. Golgotha is not a question of *whose* merits *earn* our salvation, but a rejection of the merit-earning formula itself. "The gift of God is eternal life through Jesus Christ our Lord" (Rom. 6:23), and by definition we never earn a gift. The favor was entirely *unmerited*. Even Christ's very real merits *demonstrate* God's grace to us who are in doubt. They do not *earn* it.

Furthermore, the cross demonstrates what such forgiveness—offered freely, even eagerly, and justly to the one who seeks it (after having first been sought by the one who gives it)—means. God could not safely bestow such forgiveness without also revealing the full truth. To forgive in any other way would trivialize the wrong and place the moral order itself in jeopardy. Those holding a governmental theory of the atonement were also right—up to a point. So God presented grace in a manner that burned into the universal consciousness a sense of the horror with which the redeemed must forever contemplate estrangement from God.

How then shall we characterize such an understanding of Christ's death? Atonement by disclosure? Atonement by revelation? Atonement by demonstration? Atonement by communication? Perhaps better than to label it, we should briefly attempt to qualify it.

In its essence this view proposes that *all* that was required to set up the conditions for the return of the prodigal was the disclosure of *the truth* about the nature of things—mainly the truth about sin and about God. But it also involved revealing this to all concerned in such a way that it might be perceived with the heart and not merely as objective data. The cross satisfied all these requirements.

Since the heart perceives differently from person to person, background to background, time to time, and place to place, the communication may properly employ a varying array of figures of speech to make its point. It even encourages a multiplication of metaphors. But the reality itself will always transcend any individual conceptual grasp. No human figure of speech will ever exhaust it. It is important only that those attempting to explain and understand retain a sense of the limits of language so that living truth does not become dead theory through being compressed into the mold of mere figures of speech. Theologizing has a fairly checkered track record in that respect.

Included in this truth is the fact that God has borne the full brunt of man's abuse of the freedom He gave him. God has accepted full responsibility for that creation by providing through the revelation at the cross the possibility of a new creation, and a new freedom. At-one-ment is also a creation, as we shall now see.

---
[1] See Ellen G. White, *Steps to Christ* (Mountain View, Calif.: Pacific Press Pub. Assn., 1956), p. 62.

[2] New Haven: Yale University Press, 1945, p. 2ff.

[3] *The Desire of Ages*, pp. 455, 456.

[4] When we employ the term *the cross* in what follows, it should be too obvious to mention that we are referring to the event in its larger sense. The cross as a specific instrument of torture was an accident of time and space. Had the event taken place in another time and place the means would, of course, in all probability have been different. Also, when we speak of the cross as the effect of sin that was its cause, again we are using the larger metaphor. Obviously, this specific time-place disclosure involved other more proximate causes, including choices on the part of Jesus. God selected this particular manner and occasion as the method of revealing what was in the larger sense "always so"—God always "on the cross" so long as there is sin in His universe. That truth is revealed in the cross of Calvary.

[5] Ellen G. White, *Education* (Mountain View, Calif.: Pacific Press Pub. Assn., 1952), p. 263.

CHAPTER 11

Aids to Faith

Salvation conceived in so simple terms as faith's response to God's unconditional acceptance will always seem too facile a solution to some. It is too easy—too good to be true—especially so for individuals with tender conscience and rigorous moral sensitivity. Such persons are only too aware that the Bible refers to the redeemed as those in whose "mouth was found no guile: for they are without fault before the throne of God" (Rev. 14:5). They have learned that "the condition of eternal life is now just what it always has been—just what it was in Paradise before the fall of our first parents—perfect obedience to the law of God, perfect righteousness."[1]

But they also know how difficult it is to achieve such perfection of character. They have experienced the strenuous effort, the striving every day, that it involves. Therefore, it is not surprising, that they may find the suggestion that the struggle for victory is misplaced—an irrelevant, rather disturbing idea. To them a theology that makes sinners more comfortable with their failures rather than offering them hope of success can only seem demonic. In their minds the result will surely be little less than moral chaos and an unfinished work.

Another well-known statement by Ellen White lends support to such fears. "When the character of Christ shall be perfectly reproduced in His people, then He will come to claim them as His own."[2] Putting such perfection in the context of the return of our Lord—indeed making the return dependent upon it—can only compound their apprehension. If the Lord's return is already delayed because His people are not ready, is not a teaching that seems to deemphasize "getting ready" perverse, if not downright dangerous? Especially so in the light of an increasing tendency on the part of church members to become conformed to this world? Is not such a concept a further accommodation, or at least the vehicle for it, to the current, widespread relaxed moral climate?

Well, just how good—or how perfect—*does* one have to be to be saved? This is not a meaningless question. It gains urgency by the following fact of life that we cannot ignore.

Read in one way, the statement in *Christ's Object Lessons* can only depress anyone who longs for the second coming of Jesus. It is difficult indeed to find anyone anywhere whose life meets the passage's perfectionist demands. We all fail miserably and know it as we look around us and into our own hearts. Does anyone know even a single person whose life and behavior is comparable, let alone interchangeable, with that of Jesus? And if that is so, the Lord's return is in trouble (or at least this kind of thinking about it).

But if what we have said up to this point bears any relation to reality, that is, if sin is not a *thing* but a broken relationship—and if God can restore it by a creative act of divine forgiveness—then we may be taking our cues from the wrong signals as we look around at one another and inside at our own hearts. There is no defect in the divine creation. Consider the following quotation:

> If you give yourself to Him, and accept Him as your Saviour, then, sinful as your life may have been, for His sake you are accounted righteous. Christ's character stands in the place of your character, and you are accepted before God *just as if you had not sinned.*[3] [Italics supplied.]

Ellen White does not suggest here that God or anyone else can rewrite history. We have been and done what we have been and done. And nothing can undo the past. What has been, has been—even for God. Nor does the quotation call for some kind of playacting, of God "making believe." Nor is God blind—true love never is. Rather, it involves a special kind of seeing. True love *really* sees the beloved. In this case the seeing is relational. What God perceives is a restored relation to Him.

And the restored relation is real. Those are real arms He places around us. "We may come with all our weakness, our folly, our sinfulness, and fall at His feet in penitence. It is His glory to encircle us in the arms of His love and to bind up our wounds, to cleanse us from all impurity."[4]

The result is a new and perfect creation, not an illusion. It would be an illusion if it were history that He was recreating. But since it is a new relationship, it is intensely real—because God is Creator. He can establish a new relationship. He cannot create history. It is always just what it is (though, of course, it can be seen in a different light because of new ways of perceiving things).

God's new creation provides the possibility of a new beginning. But if it does not in fact lead to a new life, it is not through some inherent fault in the creation. The problem is not in the Creator. The difficulty lies with me and my ability to accept and celebrate the creation. "Here is where thousands fail. . . . They do not take God at His word,"[5] indeed *cannot* take Him at His word without His assistance. I *cannot* believe it. *I* know myself. *I* remember what I have been and done—and those memories flood in on me and undermine my days. A prostitute finally married after plying her profession for a number of years, but the marriage lasted only a few months. When asked what happened, she replied, "There were too many memories." That's not so different from what is true of all of us. *We* continue to see our nakedness and run for our fig leaves—even if God has told us that He has forgiven us. As

Alfred Korzybski put it, "God may forgive your sins but your nervous system won't." How can we believe it?

But He understands our weakness. Again the Garden story helps us. When God found Adam and Eve in their hiding place and they told Him of their shame, He asked them, "'Who told you that you were naked?'" (Gen. 3:11, R.S.V.). They were not naked to His loving eyes. He could have said, "Throw away those foolish aprons." But He didn't. *They* needed them. Instead He fashioned for them a more effective covering to help them live with themselves in their newly experienced guilt.

God knew that, while His grace was adequate, while His forgiving acceptance had no deficiency, their faith needed assistance, so He gave them the help their faith needed. And He extends it to all of us. And those better garments also come in many sizes, shapes, and colors, as do the fig leaves.

The law itself can aid uncertain trust, that is, law as a disclosure of the way things really are. (Recall that the law as the Ten Commandments describes what God intends human creation to be.) The disclosure of the ideal assists us toward achieving that ideal—especially those of us who are a long way off.

What God "added [should we say "disclosed"?] because of transgressions" (Gal. 3:19) He revealed in part to counter transgression. If *the* original sin was distrust, leading to alienation and self-condemnation, as we suggested previously, any action or quality of experience that enhances trust, community, and self-acceptance will oppose sin.

Obedience to the Ten Commandments fosters such qualities. For example, people who do not lie to each other contribute to a social environment of trust. Husbands and wives who do not cheat on each other help to create community. We could go on through the Ten. In short, a child born into a commandment-keeping community (especially family) receives a social context favoring trust, a sense of belonging, and self-value. One who is denied such a birthright may be irreparably deprived unless . . . Thank God for surrogates.

Trust, community, and self-value are learned experiences. Early exposure to persons who manifest them may imprint such qualities in our lives. They may also be laboriously instilled by later learning situations, but experience them we must if we are to approximate in any significant way what God designed us to be. People, serving God, thus also come to attend the faith needs of other people. In this they become vehicles of divine grace. In fact, God mainly mediates His grace through such individuals.

At a lesser level, law may also foster faith. (Law exists at several levels. For example, when Paul uses the word *law* in Romans he is a good Christian Jew knowing that one can narrowly apply the Torah to the Decalogue or more broadly define it as the whole of Jewish moral teaching, including the ritual and dietary customs.) Ordinary practices and customs that provide group identity can also help to establish and preserve community. A child may be better equipped in terms of trust, community, and self-value if he knows who he is in terms of his group's customary identity marks. This may be a primary function of what we sometimes call church standards.

Law in the service of faith has its risks, of course. Obedience can all too easily be conscripted into the service of grace. That is, what God intended as an aid to me in my weakness (my weak faith) I can press into the meriting of divine favor. It is the essence of that legalism which is obedience misplaced. God is gracious by definition. No one can, or ever needs to, merit divine acceptance. The presumption that God requires our goodness in order to respond in kind is a negative answer to the question about His essential friendliness. (Recall our original question.)

There are other aids to faith. When Jesus on the night of His last meal with His disciples listened to their selfish competition for the highest place in the kingdom (their sin was pride—derived from self-doubt), He said to them, "Whosoever will be chief among you, let him be your servant" (Matt. 20:27). Then He demonstrated to them what He meant, by Himself assuming the servant role. In those words He gave a prescription for the cure of pride. If you would discover your true worth, *do* something worthwhile for others. Serving the needs of one's fellow men builds faith. The path to a sense of closeness to the heart of God leads close by the heart and needs of my brother.

Restoring the pledge—making things right—is another source of faith's reassurance. When Jesus said, "Therefore if thou bring thy gift to the altar, and there rememberest that thy brother hath ought against thee; . . . first be reconciled to thy brother, and then come and offer thy gift" (chap. 5:23, 24), He was not suggesting that we could not approach God until we had "cleaned up our act." But it is a fact of life that our "gift" will have an indifferent or even negative meaning to us as long as we have unfinished business with our brother. God may accept your gift, because He is an accepting God, but you may not be able to accept His acceptance until you have squared things away.

Unfortunately, most of the wrongs we have done cannot be righted. There is no way ever completely to undo the past. And often it is impossible even to begin the task. Certainly this is true of the false guilt we carry, where there is no clear guilt object, or even the neurotic guilt, where the object is hidden behind a false face. God's gracious acceptance extends to these guilts, as well. It may, in fact, be that there is really no other way to find freedom from such guilt.

But what, then, of our weak faith? Sometimes it can be assisted vicariously. One may find symbolic equivalents to perform that will help, at least in a measure, to set things right. Penance, unfortunately incorporated historically into an essentially unchristian merit system, at least pointed in a therapeutically valid direction. Many a person has been better able to live with himself because he had chosen to do things for others that have symbolically rectified the past, "redeeming the time."

Again, however, the danger of salvation by works lies close to the door. We must be certain that such work has its proper object—our weak faith, not God's grace.

There are other symbolic aids. We have referred to the Old Testament rituals. An Israelite on Yom Kippur watching his sins transported off into the wilderness on the head of the Azazel goat could better internalize the forgiveness God freely granted to men then as now. Israel's sacrifical system reinforced faith. Only when it became paganized into a ritual merit system did it become the "desolate" house that Jesus (and prophets before Him) rejected.

We can derive the same kind of symbolic assurance from the heavenly sanctuary depicted by the writer of Hebrews— only now more so because of the better Sacrifice (chap. 9;23), and the cosmic significance of that transcendent metaphor.

One symbol that interestingly corresponded to one of the atonement theories—mystical recapitulation—illustrates the function of symbols in enhancing faith. In Romans 6, Paul refers to immersion baptism as the possibility of our participation in

Christ's death, burial, and rising the third day. What He did we do in Him. And this would, of course, extend to His approaching the accepting throne of God at the ascension. By our identification with His victory, His becomes ours. And thus we are not only accepted by God—*we can also believe it.*

The better garments God provided in the Eden story, the aids to faith, we see nowhere better illustrated than in Jesus' parable of the lost son who came home. The father placed his own robe about his son's shoulders and his ring on his son's finger as the assurance of sonship. The father knew his son while the latter was still in his swineherd's rags. But the youth could not accept his sonship in his rags, nor could the neighbors and his brother. The robe gave the needed assurance. (We will explore this later.)

Indeed, here we find the real significance of those atonement metaphors, which eventually degenerated into theories. God aids man's weak human faith by every possible means. Christ our substitute, for example, is no charade that God plays. It is His way of assuring us of our sonship. "As I accept this My Son—so I accept all of My sons." He is a substitute, then, from our perspective, not from God's.

This is the message of Christ's advocacy for us. "And if any man sin, we have an advocate with the Father, Jesus Christ the righteous" (1 John 2:1). The word here translated *advocate* is the Greek *paraklētos,* the same word Jesus used in reference to the coming of the Comforter (John 14:16). What do *advocate* and *comforter* have in common? In the person of the Paraclete, Comforter, Holy Spirit, Jesus continued to be with the disciples always, even though He had ascended to His Father. The key term *alter ego.* (We can render *paraklētos* "alter ego" as well as "comforter" or "advocate.") The Holy Spirit on earth was Christ's alter ego—other self. Christ remained with them through the Holy Spirit. Just so we are present before the Father in our Alter Ego, Christ. We are in Him and have the assurance of our acceptance by the Father in *His* acceptance. *And thus we can believe it.*

And so God not only receives the penitent, He helps him to accept His acceptance and renders him acceptable to anyone else in God's kingdom who remembers the swineherd's former nakedness. A whole universe needs such assurance. Those complex, mysterious actions of God—the incarnation, the life, the death, the resurrection, the ascension to glory—He directed at the needs of the accepted ones, not at His own needs. The cross was for man's sake, not for God's—man's and angels'. It was the vehicle, not the cause, of divine grace.

But there is more. In the Creation story in Genesis, God, the Creator, as He brought the new world into existence pronounced it "very good," as good as if primordial chaos (the Biblical "without form, and void") had never preceded it. But He also gave the creature something to do. God entrusted him with "dominion . . . over all the earth" and commissioned him "to dress . . . and to keep" the Garden. Only God could create, but man received responsibility for maintaining the creation. And that is a point worthy of our attention.

---
[1] Ellen G. White, *Steps to Christ*, p. 62.
[2] ———, *Christ's Object Lessons*, p. 69.
[3] *Steps to Christ*, p. 62.
[4] *Ibid.*, p. 52.
[5] *Ibid.*

CHAPTER 12
Tending the Garden

Part of the apprehension those persons with sensitive conscience and a rigorous sense of moral value feel derives from their belief that being a Christian should make a difference in one's life. Saved people should be more honest, more kind, more loving, more dependable, more tolerant, more responsible, more caring, more faithful—all of these things. Friederich Nietzsche once said, "Before we can believe in redemption, Christians must look more redeemed." He was right.

In Ellen White's words:

- The atonement of Christ is not a mere skillful way to have our sins pardoned; it is a divine remedy for the cure of transgression and the restoration of spiritual health. It is the Heaven-ordained means by which the righteousness of Christ may be not only upon us but in our hearts and characters.[1]

The last phrase refers to what Christians have traditionally spoken of as sanctification. Justification, in a way, means being better off. Sanctification implies being better.

How does this change come about? Obviously, if the underlying state of brokenness—nakedness, alienation—is overcome by God's gracious, forgiving acceptance, the mechanisms for coping with that state become superfluous and unnecessary. One who stands erect as a child of God is free from the groveling incubus of his guilt. As Paul clearly says in Romans 8:

- There is therefore now no condemnation (verse 1).
- For ye have not received the spirit of bondage again to fear; but ye have received the Spirit of adoption, whereby we cry, Abba, Father. The Spirit itself beareth witness with our spirit, that we are the children of God: and if children, then heirs; heirs of God, and joint-heirs with Christ (verses 15-17).

The person who has come to accept the divine acceptance in faith has no further need of pride's status marks. And he who in that acceptance comes to accept himself also becomes free to accept others. There remains no compulsion to put others down or to exploit them to selfish ends. And from what would such a person wish to escape? The bondage is over and done. God's gracious acceptance overcomes alienation in at-one-ment. The separated is united—and the nakedness is clothed. When that is so, fig leaves are no longer necessary.

God's creative act radically alters the entire situation—even the goals of one's life. Consider that question asked earlier, "How good does one have to be to be saved?" Note its construction. Some years ago Dr. Jacob Jantzen wrote an article on medical missions for the *Alumni Journal* of Loma Linda University's School of Medicine. He headed the article with a question, "Who Gets to Go?" Not Who *has* to go?—but Who *gets* to go? Dr. Jantzen was thus calling attention to the high privilege enjoyed by one who serves God in a medical mission-field setting.

Something of this transformation is expressed in the "new creature's" attitudes. The question is not now How good do I *have* to be? But How good do I *get* to be? The forgiven Christian can now reach his newly desired goals. He really wants to be a person of integrity, honesty, loyalty, faithfulness, tolerance, kindness, loving—all of those things that gave Jesus' life its beauty and meaning. (Isn't that true of most of us? Don't we really wish to be like that—always patient, self-controlled, kind, honest?) Here's the way to reach those goals! God's grace is *enabling* grace. With guilt gone, the burden is light.

Father Flanagan's Boys Town near Omaha, Nebraska, has a sculpture of one little boy carrying another almost as big. The caption reads, "He ain't heavy, he's my brother." "My burden is light," said Jesus, because it is carried in love without the load of past guilt and self-condemnation.

Traditional Christian theology has often projected a tension between God's law and His grace, as though they were in opposition. They are opposed only when I am estranged from God. When I find myself wrapped in my Father's gracious arms, my perception of the law undergoes a transformation. I can now perceive it as a welcome expression of divine grace, as a gracious gift providing guidance to self-fulfillment, to the achievement of what I most desire out of life. In such a spirit the psalmist exulted, "I delight to do thy will, O my God: yea, thy law is within my heart" (Ps. 40:8).

Two things happen, then, when we receive God's gracious acceptance. One, with the broken relation restored the root of my sin is severed. My pride, my coping sins are cut off at their origin. And *that* is bound to have consequences. And two, accompanying the new discovery of my sonship, I have a transformed attitude toward the rules. Rather than burdensome inhibitions or strictures, they now become treasured guides to the achievement of my cherished goals—and *that* too has consequences.

Out of the primordial chaos of my life God fashions a new creation—a new beginning. I can start over again—free, totally free (if I will but believe it) of the burden of my past guilts—and am placed in a fresh new "garden," which I am given the privilege of dressing and keeping. The good news is that I can have a *new beginning* and that it can happen every day or even as many times a day as is necessary.

But the new creation does not destroy my personality. Nor does it eradicate the conditioned responses that reflect the life

I've lived up until now. If God did that He would turn me into someone else. It is *I* who am redeemed now, just as it is *I* who am eventually recreated in the resurrection—not someone else. But it is a self with new perspectives, goals, and motives, all features of the new creation. It is also *I* who am given the privilege and responsibility of caring for the new relationship.

It is a newly created garden He asks me to cultivate. I do not create it myself by hoeing weeds in the primordial chaos of my past guilt. Rather I dress and keep a *new* creation. And thus my working has as its basis a fresh start and not past guilts and failure. Therefore I proceed from a position of strength, not from one of weakness and defeat. And when those weeds of yesterday, those old habit patterns, reappear as I till the new creation—as inevitably they must—they appear as alien weeds I can attack from strength and not in weakness. Gradually they disappear forever, one by one—and I rejoice in their passing.

Grace in this setting, to repeat, is *enabling* grace. It is the power of God expressed in ever available new beginning. The new creation is available as often as needed—every day and even many times a day—new beginnings from which to grow. And how much does one *get* to grow? As much as one can in the time and circumstances allotted.

Ellen White says, "Christ looks at the spirit, and when He sees us carrying our burden with faith [remember, "He ain't heavy, he's my brother"], His perfect holiness atones for our shortcomings. *When we do our best,* He becomes our righteousness."[2] (Italics supplied.) But it is a "best" freed and strengthened by a fresh, new beginning—not weighted down by old failures!

The perfectionist point of view expressed in trying harder to become perfect is a perspective based on preoccupation with present and past failure. But by God's grace we do not have to begin our dressing and keeping in a weed patch.

In any case our holiness under God's grace is *relational.* God creates our new relationship by putting His everlasting, accepting arms around us. Our salvation rests on *His* acceptance—not on our weed hoeing. The cultivation that follows is a celebration of the new creation. Is it any wonder that the Sabbath also symbolizes sanctification (see Ex. 31:13 and Deut. 5:15)? The Sabbath expresses our gratitude—and *that's* an experience with consequences. To work at change from a celebration of gratitude rather than from a position of guilt offers the highest possibility of success.

The end point in this process points to God and not to myself. That statement in *Christ's Object Lessons* (quoted in chapter 11) need not be the basis for frustration and despair. The character of Christ being perfectly reproduced in His people so that He can come and claim them as His own is primarily a statement about a disclosure of the divine character, and only secondarily about the achievement of human goodness.

An event reported from Maoist China a few years ago illustrates this interpretation. It took place at one of those vast gatherings of Chinese young people in a stadium in Peking. On one side of the stadium several thousand Communist youth sat in a preplanned pattern. Each held a large cardboard of a single color. On signal they all held up their cards, and there appeared a huge picture of their leader. Each youth made his individual contribution—and they all together projected the portrait.

Jesus does not come when each individual follower completely replicates Him. That would be impossible. He returns when there is a collective truth adequately revealed—the truth about God. It is that disclosure that guarantees the future.

How is one saved? By God's grace alone—through faith. And what comes after? The most glorious picture of God the world has ever known—a picture given clarity and cohesion by each and all of those together who accept the new garden God creates in their lives and who dress and keep it in joyful celebration.

And how good do we *get* to be? By the grace of God as though we had never sinned, as though there had never been a primordial chaos—a perfect creation! "And God saw everything that he had made, and, behold, it was very good" (Gen. 1:31).

If we would but keep our eyes on that creation and not on our own selves and our own relative attainments (or lack of them), every day doing the best we can to dress and keep that garden, how glorious would be the expression of divine grace in our lives.

One thing more about that garden. In Eden, Adam and Eve didn't make things grow. Plants sprouted as they do now in the light of the sun and in moist, fertile soil. Just so, as we do our best to dress and keep the garden God has created, He will provide the nutrients and the water and the sun (Son?) will make it grow.

This brings us back now to the question we posed at the outset. Is Ultimate Reality hostile or friendly? Only now we can ask, "Does God wear a friendly face?" How shall we answer it?

---

[1] In *The SDA Bible Commentary* (Washington, D.C.: Review and Herald Pub. Assn., 1957), vol. 6, p. 1074.
[2] *Selected Messages* (Washington, D.C.: Review and Herald Pub. Assn., 1958), book 1, p. 368.

CHAPTER 13

You *Can* Go Home Again

Novelist Thomas Wolfe once wrote a book entitled *You Can't Go Home Again.* He intended the title to convey a fact we all have discovered who have ever tried to recapture the past: It can't be done. The only thing that does not change is change itself. Returning to the old places and trying to rekindle former friendships inevitably leaves an aching. The people either aren't there anymore or they and the places have altered so that we don't recognize them—nor they us. Better to leave them as they were, in our dreams and memories. That's the only reality they now possess.

But one return does counter Thomas Wolfe's book title, that of the sinner to the God who remains the same today, yesterday, and forever. This book is really about such a homecoming. How shall we tell it?

In our final chapter we come to the promised "un-theology" of the uniting of the separated—the at-one-ment. To call it un-theology is, of course, to be facetious. What we shall employ is the theological method of the Master Theologian Himself. Ideally, theology is clear thinking about God. And the clearest picture of God we have, Jesus conveyed by using just this method. Thus His was theology of the highest order. His method was parable—self-conscious, metaphorical, symbolical prose.

What we are going to do is simply to tell a story—one that may never have actually occurred and yet has also happened a million times and more. In one sense, then, it is fiction. Yet, in another, it is more true than history. Truth has sometimes seemed stranger than fiction, but such fiction as this can sometimes be more factual than history.

Our story derives from several parables Jesus told, especially His moving tale of the wastrel son who finally came to himself (Luke 15:11-32). It fills in some of the gaps in Jesus' narrative. (Is that presumptuous? Or is that what He intended when He called us to be His witnesses?) We relate it as Jesus *could* have presented it in a slightly different setting—and perhaps did. Who can say that He didn't? In any case, it has really happened again and again.

It attempts to summarize the answer to the question asked so often in this book about why Christ had to die—an answer, we have discovered, having to do with God's attitude toward His created children. Christ died because God loves—and that's the sum of it.

To capture the essence of that answer, it will be important to watch for certain clues as we go along. The parable covers the whole of human history (collectively and individually): the temptation and the Fall, the deception and final betrayal by evil, the unity of the Father and the Son in the cross event (how can one adequately portray the sufferings of God the Father at Calvary?), and the inevitable degradation of those who attempt to live apart from God. Above all, it seeks to convey the unchanging love of a Father totally identified with His son, even "when he was yet a great way off" and in rags, a Father who was thoughtful enough to hide the rags with His own rich robe—for the son's sake. And the homecoming!

That robe! So much of theologizing belongs to that robe. All of those classical metaphors rightly belong there. Think of the manifold ways in which God has endeavored to help us to accept in faith the reality of His gracious acceptance, and to make that acceptance acceptable to the universe that never went away—to justify (vindicate) the saving acts of the Justifier (see Rom. 3:26). Complicated books could and have been written about that covering robe, often without realizing it. But its meaning is really as simple as the story's telling.

But let us tell the story. Read it through the first time without thinking too much. Let it flow through your mind and heart. Then, if you wish, go through it again, looking for the clues.*

* * * * *

A flurry of excitement rustled through the servant's quarters like the swirl of a vagrant breeze through dry autumn leaves. Abiathar felt the excitement before he heard the news. It was Caleb's sister, Rachel, who told him, her dark eyes betraying her private elation.

"Gorgon is back."

Abiathar's eyes widened, and for a brief moment his sullen lips relaxed into the semblance of a smile. He had had few occasions to smile during the three years since his friend's departure. They had been years long with restless discontent and resentment imposed by the narrow confines of the rural valley of his father's estate. He desperately had missed Gorgon's companionship and their shared imagination of the adventure that stretched beyond the hazy mountains to the south of Elim.

Gorgon was the eldest son of Jacob the chief steward and his wife, Hannah. A strapping youth with black hair that glistened in the sun, deep-set dreamer's eyes, and full lips that

---

* This story takes place in the same period and setting as Jesus' parable. I have added place and personal names. Mainly they are incidental to the narrative except for one. That one I have derived from what Lactantius (and Milton) told us was the mysterious name of Satan—Demogorgon.

The conditions are true to life: the yearning of the younger son for the far country, the deception, his degradation, the manipulation of his stupor, the son's misperception of his father's enmity ("They know not what they do," Jesus said), the shocking discovery of what he had done, the despair, the father's continuing love and acceptance, the homecoming, and the father's reassurance. It's a story for us all. We really can go home again—no matter what we have been or how far away the country.

played easily with jesting and laughter, he was a general favorite of the servants, but especially of the younger son of old Ben Isaac, master of Elim. Friendly, outgoing, Gorgon had yet a hint of untamed colt in him as he shook his black mane and gazed at the mountains, or in the proud throw of his head and shoulders as he shouted at the sky when riding alone among the hills. One day he had abruptly left the valley, telling his father and mother only that he had to find out what lay on the other side of those mountains.

For three years no one had heard so much as a word, but now suddenly he was back. The servants clustered around him. The men pounded him loudly on his broad shoulders, and his mother and sisters kissed his cheeks and wet them with their happy tears.

Abiathar held back as befitted a son of Ben Isaac. Finally he stepped forward to greet his older, taller friend. As he searched his face, he knew that the bond was still strong between them, but he also sensed that Gorgon had changed. The other youth was heavier, with a new hardness in the lines about his mouth. His eyes seemed darker, and there was something disturbing in the way he looked at Rachel, who stood hesitantly to one side of the group.

Several days passed before the two young men were alone together. Abiathar waited until Gorgon had left the other servants and was alone along the path that led to the cluster of oaks near where his father pastured the horses. When he caught up with him, Gorgon laughed in his old way, throwing his arm around his younger friend.

"Well, Abbie boy! How've you been, kid?"

The flippant manner of address took Abiathar by surprise. Not that his being a son of Ben Isaac had ever strained their relationship, but Gorgon even from childhood had seemed aware of their differing roles in spite of the closeness of their friendship.

After Abiathar regained his composure, the words tumbled out:

"What was it like, Gorgon, on the other side, I mean? I want to hear everything. What did you do? Where were you? What did you see? Was it as exciting as we imagined?"

"Hold on," Gorgon laughed. "Hold on. There's plenty of time. I'll give you the whole thing when it's right. But it was something, I'll tell you. You'd never believe the things I saw over there—never. But first tell me about yourself. What have you been doing? The old man still riding you?"

* * * * *

During the weeks that followed, Gorgon told of the places and the sights he had seen in his travels. As he listened, Abiathar's excitement suppressed the doubts that might have risen in a more mature mind at the occasional evasive answers to his questions or the apparent inconsistencies in the narrative. Nor did Gorgon's constant emphasis on the contrast between his adventures and the dull routine of their dreary valley, and the too-ready expressions of sympathy with Abiathar's discontent, disturb him.

"Gorgon, he treats me like a child!"

"I know, kid. Bide your time. Be patient. I know what I'm talking about. Trust me."

Soon it became clear that Gorgon had no intention of remaining at Elim. It showed in his restlessness, in his inability to concentrate on his assigned tasks or to carry them out with reasonable regularity. The servants grumbled in their quarters over his new patronizing airs. Rachel began to avoid him after an encounter while working alone in the kitchen. She trembled at the thought of what her father or brothers might do if they should learn of his behavior.

The household slowly began to sense an uneasy undercurrent. Its cause was difficult to pin down at first. Rumors of minor thefts—little things, items of clothing, silver coins—began to circulate. A fine Syrian knife with a mother-of-pearl-inlaid handle disappeared from the room of Abiathar's older brother, Adab. Adab was furious, because his favorite uncle, Abinadad, had given it to him on his 16th birthday.

Then one day the chief steward reported to Ben Isaac the major loss of a bag of gold coins from the treasury. Ben Isaac was alarmed. Minor pilfering was one thing, but this . . . ! He ordered Jacob to discover the culprit and bring him to justice with all possible haste. But as he did so, Ben Isaac felt a disquieting suspicion that the culprit was none other than his chief steward's own son. It seemed more than a simple coincidence that there had arisen so much unrest at Elim since Gorgon's return.

* * * * *

The hot moonless night left no shadows where Gorgon felt his way through the courtyard to Abiathar's room. Silently he slipped through the open window to the side of the low bed on which the younger son of Ben Isaac lay sleeping. Placing his hand over the youth's face to prevent his crying out, he shook him—gently at first, then roughly. Abiathar's eyes widened in fright. Seeing the dim figure crouched over him, and feeling the hand over his mouth, he began to struggle.

"Quiet, kid. It's me," came Gorgon's hoarse whisper. "Listen carefully. I'm leaving tonight. If you're serious about wanting to go with me beyond the mountains, meet me in the morning where the old road to Achor bends around the red bluffs. I'll wait until noon for you. See you there, kid." With that Gorgon's figure faded into the darkness as silently as it had come.

For a long time Abiathar lay quietly, shaken by the experience, but also his mind now fully alert, struggling with decision. The time had come. On the one hand, he felt the pull of his childhood, the security and comfort of his home, friends, and familiar surroundings. He thought of his family—his father, not really a bad sort in spite of his strictness, and his older brother, Adab. Abiathar and his brother hadn't been close of late, but Adab had looked after him after his mother's death. On the other hand beckoned excitement and youthful adventure. "Do I want to spend the rest of my life in this dreary place," he asked himself, "when there's so much going on out there? And now's my chance."

In the morning he went to his father. You recall the story Jesus told. "And the younger of them said to his father, Father, give me the portion of goods that falleth to me." Ben Isaac remonstrated with his younger son, but Abiathar insisted. In the end the father "divided unto . . . [his sons] his living," for he knew it was useless to resist. His younger son's heart was already beyond the mountains. Abiathar joined his friend at the bend of the road, and together they went to the "far country."

* * * * *

We will pass quickly over the months of "riotous living" Abiathar spent under the tutelage of the now dissolute Gorgon—the drunken orgies, the brothels, the bars—as his inheritance dwindled. Gorgon's suggestions at first troubled him, and he frequently felt disappointed that the taste did not live up to the fantasy. Sometimes, in those aching moments that are the after-price of too much revelry, he cast a nostalgic glance at the mountains that separated him from the peaceful valley of his childhood. But those occasions became ever more infrequent as his life adapted to that of his new companions, who saw to it that he did not have many sober moments for remembering.

In Jesus' telling, the story mercifully left most of the sordid details to the imagination. But one thing He omitted from this tale He alluded to in another: the activities of the boy's father while his son lived in the "far country."

Ben Isaac deeply loved his younger son. The separation was painful almost beyond bearing. Adab watched helplessly as his father visibly aged as the months stretched into years. His once tall, erect figure began to stoop at the shoulders. His hair, though still dark with but slight frosting at the temples when Abiathar went away, had now heavily streaked with gray, and the flesh hung loosely on his once powerful arms. But it was his face that bore most strikingly the marks of his grieving. Almost daily Adab could see the lines deepen and the cheeks become more hollow and sunken. Often in the quiet of the evening as he watched the older man staring through his tears at the mountains, the vision of his father's grieving tore at his heart and fired a seething in his breast over what his younger brother's absence was doing to his father.

Ben Isaac eagerly pressed every stranger or passing caravan

for some fragment of news. Finally he commissioned his servants to go by turns beyond the mountains to find how it went with his son. He asked them not to pressure him to return, but by their presence to remind him of his father's concern. Several times Abiathar and Gorgon surprised the servants and turned on them in anger. On other occasions when he saw them hovering in the background, Abiathar tried to ignore their presence and to stifle his gnawing resentment.

* * * * *

The almost three years that had passed since Abiathar joined Gorgon at the noon meeting where the road bent around the red bluffs had taken their toll. The succession of days and nights of dissipation had marred his once youthful countenance. The sallow skin sagging beneath his eyes and around his mouth spoke of too much wine and too little sleep and the waste of his physical resources. And now, although he was not often sober enough to realize the implications of the fact, little remained of his money as well.

One hot day toward the end of the third year, Ahimihaz, the servant Ben Isaac most trusted after Jacob, his chief steward, returned to Elim in great haste. Going quickly to Ben Isaac, he bowed and said, "Master, I have come with urgent news."

"What is it, Ahimihaz? Do you bring news of my son? How is he? Speak on, man!"

"I am told your son is ill, sire. Although I did not see him, I know where he is, and those who are acquainted with him say that he is sick and in great need. I came straight away to tell you, sire, for I was sure you would wish to know. Shall I go to him? Perhaps I can minister to him and persuade him to return home."

"Thank you, Ahimihaz," the old man replied slowly, obviously shaken by the news. "No, I will go myself. I will go to him myself. Hasten! Make things ready. I shall leave at once."

Gorgon was just leaving the entrance of Ammon's gaming house when he spotted the figure of an old man walking slowly down the narrow street. His back was toward him, but, even in the dim light of the narrow passageway, Gorgon could not mistake it.

"Ben Isaac, here in Lachish," he swore under his breath.

Quickly he slipped back into Ammon's gaming house and left again by a small side door that opened into an even narrower passageway between it and the neighboring building. He darted down the alley, crossed the street behind, and slipped between other buildings, half running, stumbling over debris that littered the ancient part of the city. Finally he reached the hovel he and Abiathar shared now that their money was almost gone. Entering the doorway into the darkened room, he went to the side of the low bed on which Abiathar lay in a drunken stupor. He shook him roughly.

"Kid, Abbie, wake up!"

Half opening his rheumy eyes, Abiathar stared at Gorgon blankly. "Go . . . 'way. Don' bother me . . ."

"Come on, kid, you've got to listen. There's someone in town who's out to get you. Take this. You're going to need it."

From under his cloak Gorgon took a fine Syrian knife with an inlaid mother-of-pearl handle and pressed it into Abiathar's hand. The fingers folded around the handle weakly as the sodden brain drifted back into its stupor. A few quick moves about the room, throwing this object and that into a battered goatskin bag, and Gorgon slipped out into the night.

It was already late when at last Ben Isaac found someone who would for a price direct him to the room where his son lay. As he entered the low door, stooping to avoid striking his turbaned head on the lintel, he lifted his lamp before him and peered into the darkness of the room. A low moan escaped his lips at the scene that met his eyes in the dim circle of light cast by the flickering oil flame. The odor and the sight struck him at almost the same moment. Decaying food, human excrement, unwashed bodies, and clothing mingled with the sour smell of strong drink. Empty flasks, crumpled rags, old worn sandals, and filth littered the floor.

In the corner on what appeared to function as a bed, an inert figure lay on his back, breathing heavily through his open mouth. Even in the dim light, in spite of the dissipation that had robbed the features of their youth, Ben Isaac knew his son.

The wretch who had led him to the hovel waited until the old man uttered a cry of recognition, then faded back into the darkness.

Quickly Ben Isaac knelt beside the bed, moaning over and over, "My son, Abiathar, my son, my son. What have they done to you? Oh, my son." Abiathar's heavy breathing gave no indication of response to the old man's presence.

All through the night the aged father remained at the bedside, seemingly unaware of the passage of time or of his own weariness. His gnarled hands straightened the ragged bedclothes and softly caressed the boy's brow and cheeks, tears streaming meanwhile down his own. "My son, my poor son, could I but exchange places with you and take your sickness upon myself."

In that darkest hour just before dawn Abiathar finally began to stir and to make the inarticulate babbling of one speaking in his half dreams. Only an occasional word was audible to the anguished father as he bent low to hear the faintest sound of recognition.

"Out . . . to get . . . me."

After a time Abiathar again became silent. His only movements now were his quiet but more rapid breathing and the slow roving motion of his eyes behind their closed lids.

Suddenly his eyes opened and then focused wide in terror. In his near delirium the figure bending over him in the semidarkness took on a sinister shape. Crying out in alarm, Abiathar closed his hand tightly about the knife Gorgon had placed there. Raising it, he struck wildly at the threatening figure. Again and again he drove the knife deeply into the flapping, quivering body as it collapsed with an anguished moan and lay still on the floor. The light from the dim oil lamp shone full on the aged face of Ben Isaac where he lay crumpled on his back in a slowly enlarging pool of blood.

The sight of his father's face thrust Abiathar into full consciousness. The knife fell from his hand as he strangled the hoarse scream that forced its way to his lips. He stared in commingled horror and disbelief. "Oh, my God, what have I done?" he cried as he buried his face in his hands to blot out the nightmare.

Not only the terror of the act but the appearance of his father's face seared itself into his brain. The dim light of the lamp etched in bold relief those deep lines that spoke of months and years of grieving.

His senses reeling, Abiathar giddily glanced around the room—to the space usually occupied by Gorgon. It was empty. All of his possessions were gone. Quickly Abiathar staggered to the cache where they had hidden the little that remained of their money. It too had vanished. Nothing was left. His childhood friend had taken everything.

Abiathar turned for one last horrified look at his father lying in the blood on the floor; then, with an awful shaking, sobbing moan, he stumbled out into the night.

* * * * *

You have heard the next part of the story as Jesus told it, of how the prodigal son found himself reduced to working as a swineherd for survival, of his hunger, of how "he would fain have filled his belly with the husks" that he fed to the pigs.

What Abiathar did not know was that, although he had left his father for dead, his knife had failed to reach a vital spot. The old man hovered at the point of death from loss of blood when discovered, and remained so for many days, but he eventually recovered enough to return to his home, where he told all who inquired merely that he had fallen into the hands of an assailant. And there he continued to grieve in love for his lost son.

One day several months later he called trusted Ahimihaz to him again and once more commissioned him to inquire about his son and this time to urge him to return home.

"Tell him, Ahimihaz—tell him that I love him."

It was not easy to find the son this time. None of his former friends had seen him recently or knew where to direct the servant in his quest. But one day after weeks of fruitless searching, quite by accident (or does a higher law govern such incidents?), as he walked along a dusty road on the outskirts of

Lachish he observed a strangely familiar figure herding pigs in a nearby field. It appeared older and thinner and wore only a tattered tunic, but as Ahimihaz drew near he felt almost certain that the swineherd was Abiathar.

Approaching him, he stood for some time gazing at the face—a face so familiar and yet so greatly changed. Abiathar seemed lost in thought. Finally sensing the stranger's presence, he glanced toward him and then quickly away in the hope that his father's servant had not recognized him.

"Are you not Abiathar, son of Ben Isaac of Elim?" Ahimihaz asked uncertainly.

No answer.

"I know that you are," he continued. "I have just come from your father in Elim and I have a message for you from him. He told me to tell you that he loves you and wants you to return home."

With a look of astonishment and disbelief, Abiathar turned to the servant. "You lie. My father is dead. You have come to trick me. I know that my father is dead. I know it."

Ahimihaz stared into Abiathar's face for a long moment in silence, searching as the truth began to take form in his mind. "How could you know that, Abiathar?"

No answer.

"But it is true. Your father lives. He returned home from this land after having been, as he told us, attacked by an assailant. Sorely wounded, for a long time he lay at the point of death. But he is alive and as well as can be expected, and he has asked me to come and tell you that he still loves you and longs for your return."

The son could scarcely believe what he had heard, but as he looked into the servant's eyes, he knew that he had spoken the truth. Suddenly the sorrow, guilt, shame, and grief that he had dammed up those many months broke in a torrent of tears, and he fell to his knees before Ahimihaz, his shoulders racked with great sobs. Kneeling beside him, Ahimihaz put his arms about him as the young man babbled out the whole tragic story. The tears of both men flowed freely as Abiathar cried out his sorrow and repentance for what he had done to his father's love.

"I have sinned against God and against my father. Can I ever find mercy and forgiveness for my sin?"

"Yes, my son," the servant comforted him, "for there is only love in both the heart of God and in the heart of your father. Come home, my son." Ahimihaz returned in haste to Ben Isaac with a full report—of the finding of his son, of his present low estate, of the repentance and confession, and of the boy's fears.

At this time Ben Isaac revealed to his older son, Adab, the truth about his younger brother, and especially of the boy's sincere repentance and transformation, and of his own father-love and forgiveness. The old man spoke of his longing for the boy's return. He also called the servants together. "My son Abiathar was dead, and now he is alive!"

The news spread quickly throughout Elim. "The younger son of Ben Isaac is returning home!" All shared in the old father's rejoicing. Even the anger and resentment of Adab was softened by the new joy on his father's face.

* * * * *

Again, you have heard, in Jesus' telling, how the younger son said, "I will arise and go to my father," of his doubts along the way, of his intention to ask for a servant's place, and of the

YOU *CAN* GO HOME AGAIN

father's waiting for his son's return.

Not wishing the neighbors or the household servants to see his son as Ahimihaz had described him, in the soiled rags of a swineherd, old Ben Isaac sat daily on the veranda of the house, watching for the first indication of the boy's return. And then one day he sighted a distant speck moving slowly toward Elim. Instantly his father's heart told him that it was his son. Mentioning it to no one, he hurried down the dusty road to meet him.

Observing his father's approach, Abiathar stopped dead in fear. Silently he readied his request for a servant's place. "I . . . am no more worthy to be called thy son: make me as one of thy hired servants. . . . But when he was yet a great way off, his father saw him, and had compassion, and ran, and fell on his neck, and kissed him."

Abiathar started to stammer out the request, but Ben Isaac would have none of it. Quickly he took off his own outer robe and threw it over his son's shoulders, and taking his signet ring from his finger, he placed it on the boy's hand. Throwing his arms around him, he kissed him again and again—their tears mingling. Together they walked to the father's house, the tattered tunic of the swineherd completely covered by the father's robe.

As they accepted the greetings and cheers of the neighbors and the servants of the household, the son stood tall by his father. As they saw only the father's robe, *they* knew a son had returned. And the son looked down and saw no longer the swineherd's rags, but only the covering robe. Feeling his father's arm about his shoulders and his signet on his finger, and he knew that *he* was a son.

Together they walked into the father's house—his house—

arm in arm. There was great feasting and rejoicing in that household. All knew that what had been lost was found, and what had been dead was alive. The beloved son was home, there was a family again, and there was peace once more in the valley.